Corporate Governance

A Policy Maker's Guide to Privatisation

OECD
BETTER POLICIES FOR BETTER LIVES

Please cite this publication as:
OECD (2019), *A Policy Maker's Guide to Privatisation*, Corporate Governance, OECD Publishing, Paris.
https://doi.org/10.1787/ea4eff68-en

ISBN 978-92-64-60580-0 (print)
ISBN 978-92-64-40278-2 (pdf)

Corporate Governance
ISSN 2077-6527 (print)
ISSN 2077-6535 (online)

Photo credits: Cover © pattawee kunsrivarathai / Thinkstock

Corrigenda to OECD publications may be found on line at: *www.oecd.org/about/publishing/corrigenda.htm*.

Preface

Globalisation, technological development and increased competition have changed the conditions for many state-owned enterprises (SOEs). As a consequence, the state as an owner has had to adapt its portfolio of companies over time – reflecting also changing rationales for state ownership. The OECD does not take a position on whether or not the state should own enterprises, which should be dependent on a number of factors related to the national economy as well as domestic policy choices. However, experience shows that the SOE sector can either promote or hamper economic and social development. This depends on the extent to which SOEs operate in a sound regulatory and competition environment. It also depends on good governance – the state acting as a professional and active owner plays a key role in this regard.

Privatisation is complex and challenging, and it needs to be done right. It requires adequate preparation and planning, as well as careful execution. With over 40 years of national experiences with privatisations across the OECD area and beyond, practitioners and policy makers can learn from each other's experiences, pitfalls and successes.

Drawing on accumulated experiences and case examples, this *Policy Maker's Guide to Privatisation* provides practical advice to decision-makers on the key stages of privatisation from start to finish. It addresses fundamental questions policy makers should ask themselves before embarking on the process; steps to take to prepare a sale; steps to take during the sale – addressing key topics such as valuation and pricing; as well as what to expect post-privatisation. Newcomers to the process are likely to find it especially useful.

A number of countries are in the process of reforming the way in which they organise and manage their SOEs. They often take the internationally agreed *OECD Guidelines on Corporate Governance of State-Owned Enterprises* as a point of departure. The present Guide is an important complement to the existing consensus on state ownership practices expressed in the Guidelines. It underlines key tenants including good corporate governance, transparency, and integrity – which are all key ingredients to successful privatisations.

The OECD Working Party on State Ownership and Privatisation Practices codifies best practice and monitors SOE-related developments and policy making, and it provides a forum where policy makers and practitioners can turn to for advice. An increasing number of countries participate in this forum and use OECD experiences as inspiration for their national reform processes and privatisations.

Government investments and divestments in the corporate sector happen all the time, so the question of efficiently privatising continues to impose itself. I invite the engagement of national policy makers with the Working Party, and I recommend this Guide as an introduction to our thinking on this important subject.

Lars Erik Fredriksson
Chair
Working Party on State-Ownership and Privatisation Practices

Foreword

The rationale for developing *A Policy Maker's Guide to Privatisation* is to support the implementation of the 2015 *OECD Guidelines on Corporate Governance of State Owned Enterprises* ("OECD SOE Guidelines") and provide accompanying guidance specifically addressing best practices in privatisation. It responds to a request by the OECD Working Party on State Ownership and Privatisation Practices.

The Guide is informed by evidence gathering of recent experiences in privatisation and broadening of the ownership of SOEs and benefitted from the input of an informal task force of national experts on privatisation from Germany, Italy, Kazakhstan, Latvia, Norway, Sweden and the United Kingdom. It also draws on the conclusions of a Roundtable discussion entitled "Privatising SOEs: Recent experiences, good practices and the road ahead" held in March 2017, which brought together public officials, experts and OECD consultation partners, including the Business and Industry Advisory Committee (BIAC) and the Trade Union Advisory Committee (TUAC).

The Guide was authored by Sara Sultan Balbuena of the Corporate Governance and Corporate Finance Division in the OECD Directorate for Financial and Enterprise Affairs, with inputs from Alison McMeekin (Special section on anti-corruption and integrity in the privatisation process and Annex A). It also benefits from comments and inputs from Hans Christiansen, Korin Kane and Chung-a Park. The Guide was prepared for publication by Katrina Baker, Anne Nestour and Edward Smiley.

Table of contents

Tables

Boxes

Executive summary

Policy makers and privatisation experts agree that it is critical to "get privatisation right." A well-planned and executed transaction, backed by sound rationales, strong institutional and regulatory arrangements, good governance and integrity can have consequences on future divestment activity by enhancing investor confidence while gaining the support of stakeholders and the public. Drawing on the internationally agreed *OECD Guidelines on Corporate Governance of State-Owned Enterprises* and decades' worth of national experience across both OECD and partner economies, this *Policy Maker's Guide to Privatisation* provides practical advice to newcomers on key stages of the process from inception to post-privatisation. With global privatisation activity trending upwards, this Guide can support policy makers in their decision-making process in the years to come. The key findings are as follows:

Stage 1: Guiding principles to inform policy makers

- *Before embarking on a privatisation process, policy makers should be clear on the guiding principles and rationales underlying the transaction and should communicate these to the public.* At a high level, objectives for divestment are likely to be political and economic and require balancing trade-offs between public, private and mixed ownership. For individual privatisation "candidates", policy makers should ensure that there is a good business case, underlined by value-for-money. How the process will balance revenue maximisation and the achievement of other policy objectives should be clearly articulated, transparent and communicated at the outset of the process, including potential uses for privatisation proceeds and the fulfilment of public service obligations post-privatisation.
- *Privatisations are complex; they require transparent and credible institutional frameworks that appropriately involve stakeholders.* Decisions should be backed by high-level political support. There is a multiplicity of actors involved in the privatisation process and their respective roles and responsibilities must be well-defined. A professional and informed authority, operating at arms-length from policy making and regulatory responsibilities, should steer the execution of the transaction in close coordination with decision makers, with the early involvement of key stakeholders including the company's board and management, external advisors, employees and labour groups and in communication with the public. The overall process should benefit from high-level political support and inter-ministerial dialogue to overcome bureaucratic inertia.

Stage 2: Measures to be undertaken prior to divestment

- *Appropriate competition and market regulation should be in place prior to the privatisation. Industry or company restructuring might be necessary to ensure readiness for the sale.* Careful consideration of the transaction's impact on the company, market and wider economy should be given to ensure appropriate staging of the transaction. Sound competition and other market regulation should be in place prior to embarking on the transaction. Factors such as the size of the asset, the absorptive capacity of the market and the pre-existence of a competitive market are factors that might necessitate either industry or company restructuring. Moreover, additional steps might be necessary to evaluate the "readiness" of the company and to ensure that its equity story is in line with the stated objectives of the sale. Policy makers should also be prepared to go to parliament in case a legislative act is required to undertake the transaction.

- *The sales method will be dependent on the asset, market conditions, relative maturity of the economy and the objectives determined at the start of the process.* Policy makers should carefully consider the relative merits/demerits of various sales options, including their relative costs, staging, complexity and potential exposure to risks of corruption/illicit behaviour.

Stage 3: Organisation of the privatisation process

- *Getting appropriate advice before and during the sales process (separately for the SOE and government seller) will be necessary. Advisors should be selected according to quality, competence and experience. To avoid conflicts of interest, the separation of advisory and sales mandates is critical.* The process of privatising involves both decision-making within the state and practical measures taken by the SOEs. Depending on the size of the SOE and complexity of the transaction, these advisors will be providing legal counsel, accounting and financial advice, strategic and transaction advice, public relations advice, and communications and market research advice, among others. Special care should be taken to avoid conflicts of interest, including by separation of sales and advisory mandates.
- *Appropriate determination of company valuation is an important measure of success and is commonly based on the principle of fair market value.* An appropriate valuation will ensure the state can justify its pricing of shares to assure a fair price, achieve value for money and attract sufficient interest from investors. It will also be a key indicator to measure post-privatisation outcomes. Should a government sell at below market value (e.g. selling shares to employees at a discount, or attracting a strategic investor to facilitate technology transfer, spill overs, etc.), the reasons should be clearly identified, justified and transparent at the outset to ensure the integrity of the process. Establishing a special commission or steering group that is sufficiently independent and qualified to make an informed opinion on the valuation, as well as on the methodology used, can help to ensure objectivity in the process.
- *To avoid irregular practices, buyers should be selected based on a set of pre-qualification criteria. Bids should be transparently handled, while respecting confidentiality. Selected bids should reflect fair market value to avoid violations of state aid rules.* It is common to establish criteria for potential buyers and conduct due diligence on their financial and technical capacity, future solvency, and even corporate conduct and compliance track records. Buyers will also expect to receive a certain amount of information on the business relevant to the sale. Depending on the sales method, this will occur either through the publishing of a prospectus, or the exchange of confidential information contained in a sales book, information memorandum and/or secure data room. A minimum price can be communicated to bidders beforehand and any bids accepted should ensure fair price to avoid violations of state aid rules.

Stage 4: Steps to take post-privatisation

- *The post-privatisation phase includes wrapping up the sale, handling proceeds and establishing good governance practices if the state remains a shareholder.* Assurances to ensure adequate protection of shareholders is key. Systematic ex-post evaluation and audit are critical to independently evaluate the sale and to ensure the integrity of the process.

Chapter 1. Introduction

This chapter introduces readers to the purpose of the Guide and provides an overview of its structure, coverage, applicability and definitions. Notably, the Guide draws on the OECD Guidelines on Corporate Governance of State-Owned Enterprises as a point of departure. The chapter provides a brief overview of trends in privatisation activity over the past three decades, indicating that privatisation paradigms have shifted over time. Drawing on data from recent privatisation trends, it projects future privatisation activity will continue to rise and situates the purpose of the Guide in this context.

Purpose of this document

The rationale for developing *A Policy Maker's Guide to Privatisation* is to support the implementation of the 2015 *OECD Guidelines on Corporate Governance of State-Owned Enterprises* ("OECD SOE Guidelines") and provide accompanying guidance specifically addressing best practices in privatisation. The Guide primarily addresses the role of the state as the enterprise owner and is targeted to policy makers who are "newcomers" to privatisation or who wish to have a "refresher" on the process, key pitfalls and questions to take into consideration before embarking on a transaction or full-scale privatisation programme.

The Guide is organised in the form of an operational manual on the step-by-step process of conducting a privatisation from start to finish. It is divided into five chapters covering the key components of the privatisation process:

- Chapter 1 offers a definition of privatisation and sets the context for the Guide.
- Chapter 2 covers the guiding principles that should inform policy makers considering undertaking a privatisation process.
- Chapter 3 covers measures to be undertaken by both the company and public authorities prior to divestment to ensure success of the transaction.
- Chapter 4 covers the organisation of the privatisation process from start to finish.
- Chapter 5 covers issues that need to be considered post-privatisation.

The Guide provides case examples based on national practices. A number of "special sections" are included focusing on thematic topics such as: the timeline and process for different sales methods; privatisation through public share offerings; dealing with external advisors; and ensuring integrity of the privatisation process.

Trends in privatisation and changing paradigms

Privatisation activity today is characteristically different from privatisation activity during the so-called "golden age of privatisation", which lasted from the end of the 1980s through the early 2000s, and from the privatisations that took place between the mid-2000s and immediately following the financial and economic crisis of 2008-09. This section will briefly discuss how privatisation activity has changed throughout these periods, drawing on recent trends, as well some of the changing conditions for privatisation.

The "golden age of privatisation"

The bulk of OECD privatisation activity took place during the 1990s, which some observers call the "golden age of privatisation" (Megginson, 2016). By the middle of the 1990s, privatisation had gained momentum in most OECD member countries. In Europe, privatisation activity accelerated, especially among countries that had joined the Economic and Monetary Union (EMU), as they embarked on ambitious economic reform programmes in order to fulfil the convergence criteria of the Maastricht Treaty. OECD privatisation activities during this period were mainly through share offerings as the predominant method of sale, with a domestic retail-investor base representing a significant source of proceeds. OECD privatisations typically began with smaller assets operating in competitive sectors and then evolved to larger scale privatisations such as in telecommunications. In transition economies, governments actively pursued privatisation programmes, lasting through the early- to mid-2000s. In the latter cases, privatisation activity was seen as an opportunity to shed assets in a large state sectors, develop local capital markets and attract foreign direct investment (OECD, 2003).

According to evidence gathered on privatisation outcomes from 1989 to 2003 in both developed and developing economies, privatisation has had a generally positive overall impact in terms of increasing competition, efficiency and consumer outcomes. However, the lessons learnt from these accumulated experiences, including both successes and failures, demonstrate that economic institutions matter. This means strong rule-of-law, robust competition and enforcement, hard budget constraints, and sound governance and regulation (Guriev and Megginson, 2005).

Privatisation of the mid-2000s and through the financial crisis

Privatisation from the mid-2000s through the 2008-09 economic and financial crisis marked a different phase in privatisation activity. Following the privatisation push of the late '90s and early 2000s, many OECD governments had listed large state-owned enterprises (SOEs) on stock exchanges through public offerings; whereas others were sold to strategic investors. In both cases most of the privatisation activity was characterised by the state remaining a majority or significant minority owner of shares. These partially state-owned enterprises benefited from performance and efficiency improvements through the disciplines of stock market listing or private ownership. On the other hand, mixed ownership allowed the state to maintain strategic participation in companies for which there remained a rationale for continued state ownership.

During this period, privatisation activity in the OECD area was mainly dominated by the partial or tranche-wise sell-off of large SOEs in the utilities and/or network industries, where state ownership remained. The sequential approach was justified mostly by the size of the enterprises but also market conditions. Despite a dip in privatisation activity among OECD countries, this period was also characterised by a marked rise in privatisation transactions outside of the OECD area, with partial privatisation transactions carried out in large emerging economies, including China and Russia. For this reason, some observers have characterised this period as giving rise to a "new privatisation landscape" (OECD, 2009; 2010) in which a large number of enterprises were subject to privatisation processes but were not transferred to private ownership in their entirety.

With the benefit of hindsight, most of the remaining secondary or tertiary offerings were delayed when markets stabilised and the enterprises in question established a financial track record. Consequently, many of these transactions have taken many years – and in a number of OECD countries are still ongoing.

Privatisation of today and the near future

The privatisation activity of today and the near future is likely to be different from the previous period. A 2018 OECD report indicates that global privatisation activity is trending upwards following an initial drop in the wake of the international financial crisis. From 2008 through 2016, privatisation revenues have more than doubled from around USD 110 billion in 2008 to USD 266 billion in 2016 (OECD, 2018). This development was accompanied by a marked regional shift from privatisation activity mainly originating in European economies to emerging economies. Most of the shift is due to the growing magnitude of privatisation within China. But it also reflects the fact that governments, already under pressure to raise fiscal revenues, have also reassessed the role of the state in the commercial economy and have increasingly chosen to make the best use of the opportunities for privatisation that have emerged with internationalisation, market de-regulation and technological progress.

In terms of sectorial distribution, privatisation within the OECD area (representing mainly European economies) has, in recent years, been tilted toward the financial and real estate sectors. This mostly reflects governments' efforts to disengage from financial institutions that had been partly nationalised and/or recapitalised (including through the issuance of non-voting shares) with a continued government stake as a result of the economic and financial crisis. A number of governments have privatised real estate management firms and/or unincorporated real estate portfolios. Other important sectors include public utilities, reflecting a completion of privatisation transactions initiated in earlier phases (see above), thanks to: increased competition from the private sector; market-based regulation which, in the eyes of many governments, gradually eroded the rationale for state ownership; and improved market conditions.

This period also marks a change in the preferred privatisation method among many OECD economies. The privatisation activity of today, apart from a few notable initial public offering (IPOs) or secondary public offering (SPOs), is mainly centred on private sales. This largely reflects an increased preference for equity capital observed for private companies as well.

This period is also notable in that a decade after the adoption of the OECD SOE Guidelines, the professionalisation of state ownership across the OECD area has, arguably, had an impact on the dynamics of privatisation. For example, increasingly professionalised ownership entities are more involved in an advisory capacity to the government and have served to inform the privatisation process. This has also helped to balance out the role and influence of external advisors in the privatisation process.

Privatisation dynamics have also changed through the digitalisation of the economy more generally. Digitalisation has allowed the state as owner to share information more broadly on privatisation programmes and arguably attract interest from a broader, more international, group of buyers beyond the "traditional" domestic retail buyers. Digitalisation allows for more complete exchanges of information, such as through virtual data rooms, and greater transparency on the privatisation process towards stakeholders and the public.

As for emerging economies, many with large state sectors, which are expected to grow briskly, divestment activity is likely to grow in the coming years. This upward trend will be further supported by significant (but not massive) privatisation activity in a number of OECD economies. It is yet to be seen whether the emergence of the "green" economy will have an impact on public utilities and gas/energy companies that remain in public ownership. For these reasons and continuing fiscal challenges in both industrialised and emerging market countries, some observers (Megginson, 2017) posit that continuing privatisation programmes will remain a central issue for policy makers for many years to come.

Figure 1.1. Changing paradigms for privatisation

The privatisation paradigm for OECD economies has shifted and future privatisation activity will be led by emerging economies.

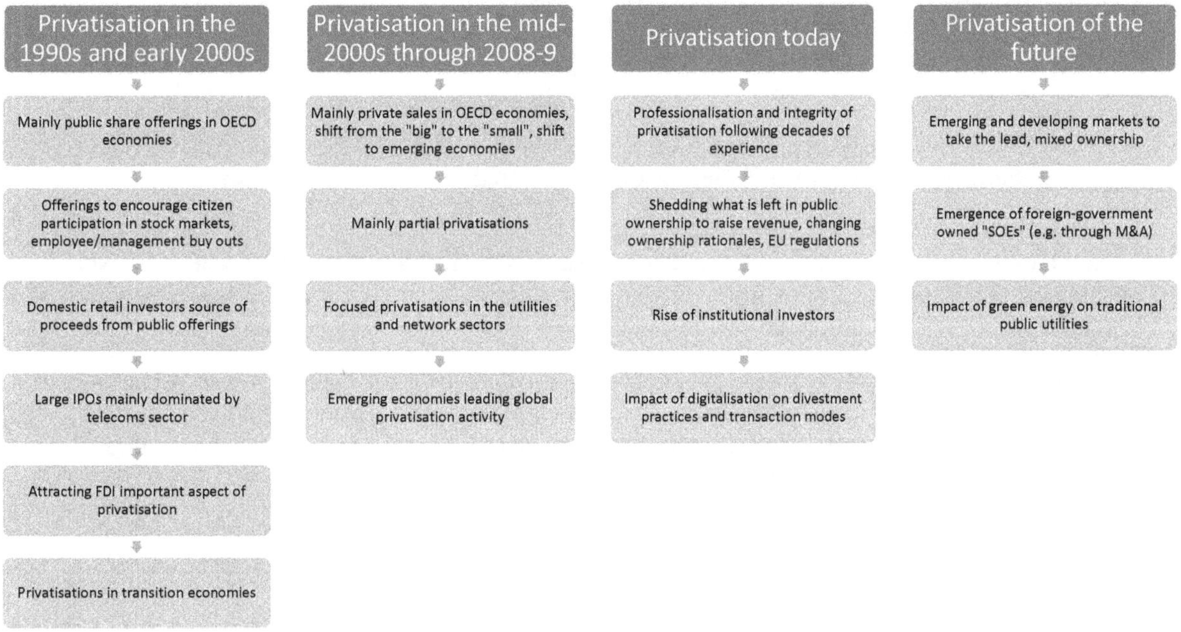

OECD Guidelines on Corporate Governance of State-Owned Enterprises as a point of departure

This Guide is addressed to governments that are committed to implement the OECD SOE Guidelines, and that have undertaken the foundational structural reforms necessary to implement their main policy tenants. This means that regulation has been separated from ownership, independent regulatory authorities are in place and a certain degree of market liberalisation has occurred. It is likely that the Guide will also be a useful reference point for those who are undergoing SOE reform in parallel with structural reforms.

The OECD SOE Guidelines do not pronounce themselves on the merits or demerits of privatisation and they do not place judgement as to whether certain activities are better placed within public or private ownership. However, the OECD SOE Guidelines serve as an important guidepost for the state acting as an owner to manage more effectively their responsibilities as company owners, thus helping to make state-owned enterprises more competitive, efficient and transparent. Moreover, ensuring the good corporate governance of SOEs will be an important factor in ensuring success of an eventual privatisation, as it is a prerequisite for economically effective privatisation, enhancing SOE valuation and hence bolstering the fiscal proceeds from the privatisation process (Box 1.1).

Box 1.1. OECD Guidelines on Corporate Governance of State-Owned Enterprises

Chapter I. Rationales for ownership: The state exercises the ownership of SOEs in the interest of the general public. It should carefully evaluate and disclose the objectives that justify state ownership and subject these to a recurrent review.

Chapter II. The state's role as an owner: The state should act as an informed and active owner, ensuring that the governance of SOEs is carried out in a transparent and accountable manner, with a high degree of professionalism and effectiveness.

Chapter III. State-owned enterprises in the marketplace: Consistent with the rationale for state ownership, the legal and regulatory framework for SOEs should ensure a level playing field and fair competition in the marketplace when SOEs undertake economic activities.

Chapter IV. Equitable treatment of shareholders and other investors: Where SOEs are listed or otherwise include non-state investors among their owners, the state and the enterprises should recognise the rights of all shareholders and ensure shareholders' equitable treatment and equal access to corporate information.

Chapter V. Stakeholder relations and responsible business: The state ownership policy should fully recognise SOEs' responsibilities towards stakeholders and request that SOEs report on their relations with stakeholders. It should make clear any expectations the state has in respect of responsible business conduct by SOEs.

Chapter VI. Disclosure and transparency: State-owned enterprises should observe high standards of transparency and be subject to the same high quality accounting, disclosure, compliance and auditing standards as listed companies.

Chapter VII. The responsibilities of the boards of state-owned enterprises: The boards of SOEs should have the necessary authority, competencies and objectivity to carry out their functions of strategic guidance and monitoring of management. They should act with integrity and be held accountable for their actions.

Source: OECD (2015), *OECD Guidelines on Corporate Governance of State-Owned Enterprises*, 2015 Edition, OECD Publishing, Paris. http://dx.doi.org/10.1787/9789264244160-en.

A number of countries are in the process of reforming the way in which they organise and manage their SOEs; they have in many cases taken international best practices such as the OECD SOE Guidelines as points of departure or even benchmarks. This Guide assumes that as a point of departure the government must already work towards:

- professionalising the state as an owner
- making SOEs operate with similar efficiency, transparency and accountability as good practice private enterprises
- ensuring that competition between SOEs and private enterprises, where such occurs, is conducted on a level playing field.

Applicability and definitions

The Guide is applicable to the privatisation of entities that are already pursuing economic activities or are expected to do so after privatisation. Moreover, to limit the scope of issues to be addressed, it only applies to privatisation of corporate assets in which there is a significant change in government ownership or control. The term “privatisation” covers full or partial divestment of incorporated assets by governments. This may take numerous forms, including listing in stock markets (through IPOs); trade sales to private firms; management buy-outs; and the issuance of stocks or convertible bonds by the SOEs themselves. Conversely, the sale of physical assets by SOEs or the transfer of activities to the private sector through instruments such as concessions and public-private partnerships would normally not be considered privatisation.[1] Moreover, the privatisation or liquidation of assets which take the form of state property but would not be subject to corporatisation are not included in the scope of this report.

Notes

[1] For good practice guidance related to the transfer of activities to the private sector through instruments such as concessions and public-private partnerships, further guidance can be found in the OECD Recommendation on Principles for Public Governance of Public-Private Partnerships and accompanying best practice guides including the “PPP Reference Guide”.

References

Guriev S. and Megginson W. L. (2005), Privatization: What Have We Learned?, ABCDE conference, St Petersberg, January 2005.

Megginson, W. L. (2017), Privatization Trends and Major Deals in 2015 and 2016, in Privatisation Barometer.

Megginson W. L. (2016), Privatization, State Capitalism, and State Ownership of Business in the 21st Century. Foundations and Trends in Finance, vol. 11, no. 1–2, pp. 1–153, 2017.

OECD (2018), *Privatisation and the Broadening of Ownership of SOEs: Stocktaking of National Practices*, https://www.oecd.org/daf/ca/Privatisation-and-the-Broadening-of-Ownership-of-SOEs-Stocktaking-of-National-Practices.pdf.

OECD (2015), *OECD Guidelines on Corporate Governance of State-Owned Enterprises*, 2015 Edition, http://dx.doi.org/10.1787/9789264244160-en.

OECD (2010), *Privatisation in the 21st Century: Summary of Recent Experiences*, https://www.oecd.org/daf/ca/corporategovernanceofstate-ownedenterprises/43449100.pdf.

OECD (2009), *Privatisation in the 21st Century: Recent Experiences of OECD Countries: Report on Good Practices*, January 2009, https://www.oecd.org/daf/ca/corporategovernanceofstate-ownedenterprises/48476423.pdf.

OECD (2003), *Privatising State-Owned Enterprises: An Overview of Policies and Practices in OECD Countries*, OECD Publishing, Paris, https://doi.org/10.1787/9789264104099-en.

Chapter 2. Guiding principles

This chapter discusses the guiding principles that should inform policy makers when considering a privatisation programme or transaction. It discusses how policy objectives are identified and articulated, drawing on lessons learnt from national privatisation experiences; underlines how a transparent and credible institutional framework with high-level political support and early stakeholder engagement can support the privatisation programme; and outlines how best to sequence the process to build credibility and support.

The decision to privatise a state-owned enterprise (SOE) is complex and influenced by evolving governmental priorities, political cycles and changing paradigms about the merits/demerits of public ownership. It is also impacted by previous privatisation experiences, evolving public discourse on the matter and other factors. Although the decision-making process is complex and never completely divorced from political considerations, this chapter provides tools to the policy maker on how best to anchor the process to ensure credibility, transparency and integrity, while avoiding discretionary decision-making.

This section discusses the guiding principles that should inform policy makers when considering a privatisation programme or transaction. It discusses how policy objectives are identified and articulated, drawing on lessons learnt from national privatisation experiences; underlines how a transparent and credible institutional framework with high-level political support and early stakeholder engagement can support the privatisation programme; and outlines how best to sequence the process to build credibility and support.

Identifying and articulating policy objectives

Rationales for privatisation

Privatisation objectives are multiple, and at times conflicting, and their relative importance has varied across countries, and even within the same country they have changed over time. Although there is no single approach to privatisation, the rationale for divestment is inextricably linked to the rationales for ownership (See Figure 2.1).

These rationales should be made transparent and based on clear criteria, which can help to avoid overly "subjective" decision-making, while also ensuring a good business case and value for money. Ensuring value for money will necessarily require balancing revenue maximisation with other policy goals, which are often immaterial but important to define in advance of the process. Cited examples of rationales for divestment often include:

1. rationale for government intervention no longer present (e.g. government intervened because of a market failure and that market failure is no longer present)
2. raising revenue for the national treasury either to reduce debt or to raise expenditure
3. improving economic or sectoral economic performance
4. enhancing the efficiency of the individual SOE
5. developing national stock exchanges
6. diversifying corporate ownership and/or attracting outside investment
7. attracting a strategic or foreign investor
8. opening up markets for competition and improving service delivery.

Where an ownership policy exists, the privatisation of an SOE will typically be justified by the fact that this company no longer falls within the rationale for state ownership established by the policy. A state enterprise ownership policy provides SOEs, the market, and the general public with predictability and a clear understanding of the state's overall objectives and priorities as an owner. The ownership policy should ideally take the form of a concise, high-level policy document that outlines the overall rationales for state enterprise ownership (Figure 2.2). According to the annotations of the *OECD Guidelines on Corporate Governance of State-Owned Enterprises* ("OECD SOE Guidelines"), the state, where relevant, should also include information in the ownership policy on its policy and plans regarding the privatisation of SOEs. The rationale for government ownership should be made clear and transparent and should be restated at certain intervals, with measurable indicators for determining if the stated rationale is still applicable (e.g. market failure).

Figure 2.1. Rationales for ownership and divestment: A balancing act

Rationales for divestment and public ownership are inextricably linked and should be balanced.

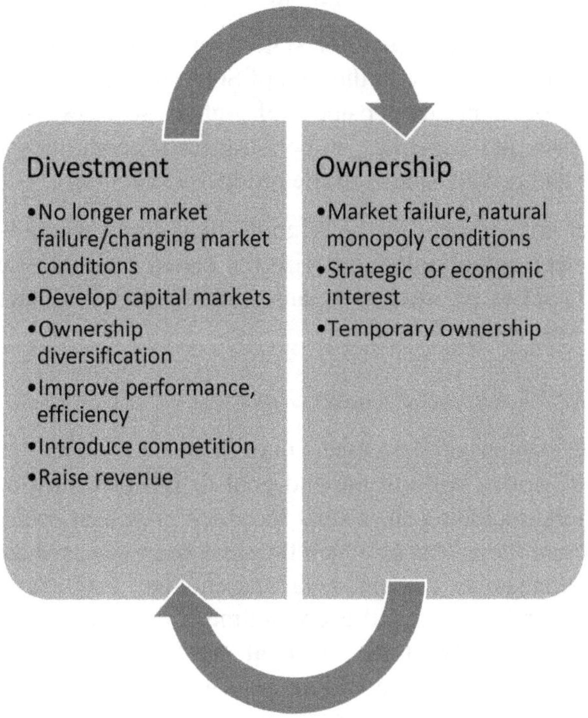

Figure 2.2. What is an ownership policy?

Privatisation is typically justified when a company no longer falls within the rationale for state ownership established by a state ownership policy.

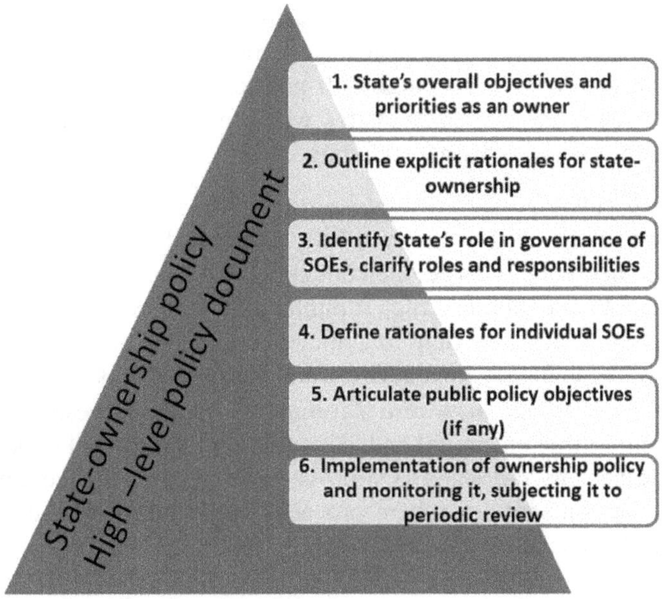

In mature economies, the rationales for state ownership are mostly limited to the need to remedy market failures and to provide goods and services for which there is no likely private supplier. Privatisation has often been motivated by changing market conditions where SOEs operate and the entrance of private competitors.

In emerging economies, the rationales for state ownership are sometimes defined more broadly and may for instance relate to the role of SOEs in national development strategies or in the provision of a broader palette of public services, safeguarding national ownership of enterprises and, especially in post-transition economies, an ongoing effort to rebalance the public and private shares of the productive economy.

Countries also differ with respect to the "rigour" they apply when assessing what to do with an SOE no longer complying fully with the stated rationale for ownership. Many governments would tend to see such companies merely as "candidates" for privatisation (see also section on sequencing below).

Rationales for mixed/broadened ownership

In some cases the divestment of state assets may fit into a broader "mixed ownership" or (partial) "divestment" policy without the end goal of full privatisation. This will depend on a number of factors, including the extent to which privatisation is accepted as part of the public discourse and the extent to which the state has expressed the policy as part of a broader economic strategy to remain as a shareholder. For example, the state may maintain residual ownership to signal a commitment that the government is willing to share the residual risk with investors. The dual involvement of the state and a private company as shareholders can balance various priorities. For example, the involvement of a private industrial shareholder in the company can bring in changes to the operational strategy and management of a company.[1] At the same time, state involvement can lower transaction costs in areas where the enterprise continues to deliver on public policy objectives of a "social" nature through effective regulation. The presence of private investors may allow for investments in longer-term and more risky projects, especially in certain capital intensive, and sometimes uncertain, investment projects, such as in the oil or mining sectors. The presence of a government shareholder may balance out the short-termism of private investors concerned primarily with maximising shareholder value, while the market-orientation of private investors may balance out government pressures to reap short-term dividends associated with political or fiscal cycles. A recent OECD study (OECD, 2016) found that many states which pursued mixed ownership or partial divestment did it for various reasons, including:

- *Remain shareholder for strategic reasons:* Retaining state shareholdings in a company can ensure that it is not fully controlled by foreign or other investors that could theoretically target the company for a takeover. This can also allow the government to maintain leverage if public policy objectives are still carried out by the company. It can also help to achieve certain strategic policy objectives, such as maintaining company headquarters and R&D activities in the country.
- *Free up capital and maximise revenue*: A partial divestment can allow the government to free up capital and, depending on the market conditions, maximise revenue, especially if it leads to improvements in performance, thus increasing the value of the company, or where proceeds could be maximised by sale in more than a single tranche.

- *Attract private capital and financial resources to companies:* Mixed ownership of SOEs permits the government to share risk with private investors and attract financial resources to SOEs.
- *Drive performance improvements through market discipline:* A number of studies show that on average in the long-run, mixed-ownership listed companies yield better returns in terms of profitability, output and efficiency than companies remaining unlisted and 100% state-owned.
- *Strengthen the local stock market:* Countries with under-developed capital markets may list SOEs as a means to develop capital markets. In countries with well-developed stock markets, the stated motivation may be more oriented towards encouraging citizen participation in the stock market, by increasing attractive investment opportunities.
- *Improve the governance and transparency of SOEs*: Where private ownership is introduced through a public share offering, the listing requirements of the stock market often raise the governance and transparency of SOEs. This includes: requirements for audited financial statements which, if not in place prior to listing, may improve transparency around SOE operations; and introducing requirements for independent directors. Non-state shareholders may have better abilities and incentives to monitor and exercise effective control over management. Listing debt would achieve similar goals, even if to a lesser degree.
- *Free SOEs from public spending limits and state intervention:* In some cases introducing an outside shareholder has also reportedly given the company increased autonomy from the state in the management of the enterprise's affairs, while also freeing up the SOE from public spending limits.

Tools to make an informed decision and setting sales objectives

Countries undertaking a privatisation programme need to have clear objectives for what they want it to achieve. Objectives for divestment are likely to be both political and economic and often require trade-offs between various interests which influence the nature of the reform that is undertaken. Still, the competent authorities have a number of tools at their disposal to make an informed decision about privatisation. This includes carrying out a competition assessment; undertaking a cost-benefit or value-for-money assessment; carrying out periodical reviews of the public ownership portfolio; and establishing clear policies for the use of privatisation proceeds. This section provides a brief (non-exhaustive) overview of tools used in some jurisdictions.

Competition assessment

Consensus after decades of privatisation has been that competition and other market regulation should necessarily be in place prior to privatisation. This involves evaluating the market structure and the degree of competition. Since privatisation is often a component in a larger set of liberalising, competition-enhancing reforms, some increased exposure to competition can contribute to better privatisation outcomes or even determine whether privatisation will result in an optimal outcome. Doing a competition assessment can help to evaluate whether the state's presence in the marketplace has anti-competitive effects, whether any such effects are inevitable (or the policy objectives could be achieved in a less distortionary way) and how to assess the costs of such distortions to enable the government to make an informed policy choice about privatisation or other market correcting measures. The OECD's Competition Assessment Toolkit provides guidance in this regard.[2]

Privatisation in and of itself has also served as a vehicle to enhance competition by providing an opportunity for sector restructuring, where governments replace state-owned monopolies with several competing firms and, in the case of the network industries, establish third-party access and competition rules. If increased competition is one of the objectives of privatisation, a first and important step is to evaluate the extent to which divestment will help to achieve this goal as well as the broader benefits to the competition environment and consumers.

Some jurisdictions apply a "yellow pages rule" which establishes that if a private company exists in a certain market, then the state should exit that market (See case example from Kazakhstan in Box 2.1.). Chapter 3 of this Guide provides more detailed coverage of this topic.

Box 2.1. Case example: Competition considerations in Kazakhstan

"Yellow Pages Rule" restricts state ownership where there is a private competitor

In Kazakhstan, the Yellow Pages Rule is incorporated into the Entrepreneurial Code of 2015 and limits state involvement in the market economy. In particular, Article 192 of the Entrepreneurial Code provides for the cases when the state may participate in economic activity. It states that "the state shall participate in entrepreneurial activity in the following cases":

1. absence of another opportunity of ensuring national security, defence capability of the state or protection of societal interests
2. use and maintenance of strategic objects held in state ownership
3. performing activities in the fields related to the state monopoly
4. performing activities by organisations established for analysis of effectiveness and preparation of proposals on improving public policy
5. absence of the relevant goods (works, services) market of an entity (entities) of private business, performing production or sale of the like or interchangeable good (work, service)
6. performing activities by established affiliated persons of the national managing holding "Baiterek", created as part of the measures on optimisation of the system of management of development institutions, financial organisations and development of the national economy
7. in cases directly foreseen by the Entrepreneurial Code, laws of the Republic of Kazakhstan, decrees of the President or Government Resolutions of the Republic of Kazakhstan.

In sectors where SOEs are already active, if there is a private company, which can provide the same goods, works and services, then the law stipulates that the state should leave this field by transferring the SOE to the competitive market through privatisation, PPP or concession.

Source: Submission by Kazakh authorities.

Ex-ante evaluation of privatisation objectives

Prior to privatising an SOE, the government will need to carefully consider possible impacts that the transaction might have on the company, the market and the wider economy. The types of assessments carried out will need to assess: costs and benefits, both to the company and the wider market and economy; value for money of the transaction; and timing and risk assessments. Some questions that policy makers may want to consider include:

- Will privatisation bring about improvements to efficiency, performance, and public service delivery (if applicable)?
- Does it make sense to privatise before making any changes to the market structure and introducing market regulation? What changes are required within the company? (These issues are considered in more detail in the Chapter 3 discussion on pre-privatisation industry and company restructuring).
- Is there value for money for the government? For example, will the method of transaction ensure an optimal use of resources to achieve the intended outcome? Some governments report that a "value-for-money assessment" is required before undertaking a privatisation transaction. The transaction will also be assessed by the national audit office or other competent authority ex-post. When considering value-for-money, beyond the value of the transaction, have other considerations been made? These could include, for example: transfer of future liabilities; absence of future government funding; and efficiency gains realised by transferring ownership from the public to the private sector (see Box 2.2).
- Will the transaction fulfil certain other policy goals (i.e. beyond value-for-money), if they were clearly articulated in advance as among the guiding principles/rationales for privatisation? These could include, for example, the ability to attract a strategic investor from another country or to pass on residual liabilities to an investor.

Box 2.2. Setting sales objectives: Case example from the United Kingdom

Examples of recent sales objectives in the United Kingdom

Lloyds Banking Group:

The government's primary sales objective of its 43% stake in Lloyds Banking Group was to return the company to full private ownership, achieving value for money for the taxpayer and recovering as much of the initial investment as possible.

Green Investment Bank:

The government's primary objectives were to achieve value for money for the UK taxpayer and reclassification of GIB to the private sector. It was the government's intention that GIB should continue to focus on green sectors and play a role in accelerating the United Kingdom's transition to a more sustainable low-carbon economy.

Royal Mail:

The government secured the universal postal service for the benefit of all users by ensuring Royal Mail's future through the introduction of private sector capital and associated disciplines. This was achieved by:

- delivering a sale of shares in Royal Mail within parliament
- creating an employee share scheme that, as decided by parliament, will lead to at least 10% of the company being in employee ownership, to drive stronger staff engagement
- delivering a financial outcome for the taxpayer, which when considered in the context of the overarching policy objective, represents overall value for money.

Eurostar:

The government's main objective was to maximise value for money by:

- maximising net proceeds (sale proceeds less transaction costs)
- maximising certainty of deal closing
- minimising post-sale residual risks to the government.

Source: Submission from UK authorities.

Specific assessment for universal service obligations

Where the privatisation will have a potential impact on the delivery of universal service obligations, policy makers should undertake a specific assessment to ensure that the transaction does not undermine the delivery of such services and if transferred to the privatised entity, that fundamental principles of quality, affordability, accessibility and universality are guaranteed. This assessment should take into account long-term assessments on costs and efficiency.

Periodic review of government ownership

It is considered good practice to review governments' enterprise ownership rationales at regular intervals. Practices for undertaking these reviews vary across jurisdictions and can inform the decision-making process for divestment. Some methods are described as follows:

- Where ownership policies exist, some countries review the rationale for ownership/divestment through a regular or as-needed review of their framework for state ownership. Germany, for example, conducts a two-yearly review of its portfolio of SOEs during which it must be justified why each company shall remain in state ownership, after which failing companies will be privatised.
- In the absence of a state ownership policy, divestment is often considered when assessing individual SOEs' fulfilment of their objectives. In the case of Israel for example, each SOE's fulfilment of objectives, status and ownership rationale is periodically reviewed.
- In other jurisdictions, such reviews occur in the context of annual aggregate SOE reporting or in the preparation of broader development, investment and financial planning programmes (as is the case for Turkey).
- In Norway, the government has conducted privatisation "readiness reviews" for companies regardless of whether there is an actual wish to privatise the asset. This is useful in order to determine how prepared a company is for privatisation concerning e.g. reporting routines, internal control, corporate governance, operational and financial efficiency, and for the owner and/or the company to take action if needed (See also Chapter 3 for more on the "readiness review").

In general, the owner needs to be aware of the SOEs in its portfolio and their readiness for privatisation and it needs to be clear on its own objectives with the companies. For example, if an SOE operates strategic infrastructure, privatisation may not be a viable exit strategy; whereas, in other cases the state may currently be the owner of shares, but has clearly stated in its ownership policy that it plans to divest it shares, thus signalling its objectives to the market. As such, being consistent and having a clear overview of the state's portfolio will be important precursors for the success of future privatisation transactions.

Uses for privatisation proceeds

Prior to embarking on the privatisation process, the government must decide on the various rationales behind the privatisation, the uses for privatisation proceeds and, where relevant, the appropriate investment vehicle or fund through which privatisation proceeds will be channelled (e.g. sovereign wealth, infrastructure, pension, or innovation fund). This can also help ensure that stakeholders and the public at large see the benefits of the reform and possibly secure broader public support for privatisation (See Box 2.2). The provisions governing the use and treatment of privatisation proceeds can also serve as a vehicle for enhancing transparency and accountability and achieving a balance between the fiscal and efficiency drivers of privatisation. As mentioned above, one of the stated rationales for divestment often quoted by governments is the need to raise revenue either to reduce the government debt, or to reinvest to meet other policy priorities such as funding of social safety nets and other public services (e.g., health and education, worker retraining) and/or funding deficits. More examples are provided in Box 2.3 and in Chapter 5 of this report.

Box 2.3. Privatisation proceeds to support other economic goals

Privatisation proceeds can be reinvested to meet other policy priorities. In France, for example, the government announced a substantial state assets sales plan (USD 12 billion). The proceeds of this operation are planned to go towards a planned fund for innovative start-up companies.

The French government announced a EUR 10 billion (USD 12 billion) state assets sales plan in July 2017. The proceeds of this operation are planned to go towards a planned fund for innovative start-up companies. As the first step of the plan, the government conducted the sale of a 4.5% stake in gas utility Engie SA (ENGIE.PA) for EUR 1.53 billion (USD 1.82 billion) in September 2017. The state remains the leading Engie shareholder, with 24.1% of the capital and 27.6% of the voting rights.

Source: Submission by French authorities.

Establishing a transparent and credible institutional framework with high-level political support

Privatisation transactions are complex, requiring extensive planning and preparation. Depending on the type of assets being sold, privatisation of SOEs can give rise to a host of policy questions and decisions that need to be addressed prior to sale. These include decisions such as when and how to restructure the SOEs that are slated for sale, hiring of advisors, timing, the decision as to who should lead the process, the approach to labour issues, the size of stake for sale, the method of the transaction, and how fast the asset should be sold. There also needs to be agreement up front on the decision-making process, for example at which stage are ministers consulted, and how the wider sales process will be governed to make sure all necessary stakeholders are involved. For this reason, the institutional framework for decision-making and management of privatisation policy and the development of a clear road map are critically important for the smooth execution of privatisation policies and for ensuring the programme's success. It should be noted that even where political support is garnered, the privatisation transaction may or may not go through. This will depend on a host of issues including the readiness of the company, the market conditions, or other considerations, which may affect the decision-making process.

Institutional arrangements often involve various levels of government

The multiplicity of actors involved in a privatisation, each with their own vested interests, means that the process should be well organised with a strong institutional framework. Otherwise, transactions can be delayed and the absence of a clear policy on staging and sequencing (such as company or industry restructuring) can create uncertainty and undermine the credibility of the programme.

Many governments structure the institutional framework involving various levels of government as part of a hierarchy of responsibilities. At the top, the process is backed by political commitment at the highest level to move the process forward. Some countries note that dynamism in the privatisation process can be found when there is a major change in government or following an election cycle (Box 2.4).

On a second level, an inter-ministerial dialogue/committee can support the process by serving to resolve bureaucratic inertia and inter-institutional rivalries. The dialogue/committee can also identify relevant policy questions, develop appropriate responses and ensure that all the relevant issues have been addressed prior to going to the market (Figure 2.3).

Figure 2.3. Typical institutional arrangements for a privatisation transaction

Various levels of hierarchy involved in the institutional arrangements for privatisation.

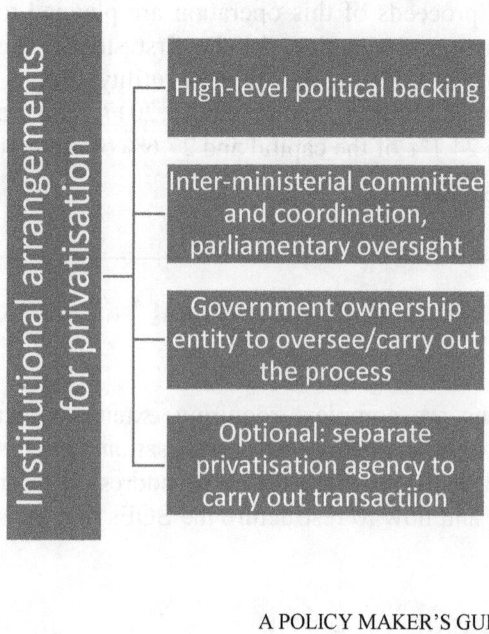

At a third level, the process needs to be supported by a professional (preferably centralised) ownership entity or other competent authority (e.g. privatisation agency) giving structure to the privatisation process and ensuring that the transaction can stand up to various levels of scrutiny. This will help to ensure that once a decision is made, the process is run effectively and ministers are engaged at the right time on the right matters. As a separate issue, a well-governed and transparent decision-making structure helps to avoid unwarranted political interference.

An example can be drawn from recent past experience in Lithuania. During the country's active privatisation programme, a three-level hierarchy of responsibilities to its privatisation processes was established. Overall political oversight was exercised by the Privatisation Committee which consisted of representatives of government ministries and parliament. The Ministry of Economy, which is also responsible for coordinating the state ownership policy, was the government agency charged with implementing the privatisation policy for state property. The actual process of privatisation, as well as temporary asset ownership, was steered by the state-owned *Turtos Bankas* (Property Bank) which (at the time) also hosted the Governance Coordination Centre (a coordination body for the oversight of the SOE portfolio not slated for privatisation).

Box 2.4. Privatisation must benefit from a high level of political backing: Example from Norway

For the privatisation to be a success, it must benefit from a high level of political backing. In Norway, the privatisation process is often initiated when there is a major change in government or following an election cycle. It also requires interaction with Parliament to get approval for the privatisation transaction and coordination with relevant parts of government before carrying forward the transaction. The process in Norway consists of four steps, initiated by a "White Paper" submitted to Parliament and concluded by a decision made by the responsible ministry and coordinated with other parts of government. The process is as follows:

- *White Paper on State Ownership:* Usually after each election (approximately every 4th year) or change in government, the Ministry of Trade, Industry and Fisheries (where the centralised ownership unit is placed) outlines on behalf of the whole of government the state's ownership policy in a so-called "White Paper on State Ownership". This White Paper identifies the overall objectives for state ownership and for each individual company that the state owns. The ministry submits the White Paper to Parliament.
- *Annual state-budget approval process:* The annual state budget includes specific requests for approval by the Parliament of mandates to fully or partially dispose of shareholdings (within the framework of the White Paper). The mandate is issued to the ministry that is delegated the responsibility for managing the ownership of the company in question.
- *Following mandate, decision requires ministry approval:* The ministry that is delegated the responsibility for exercising ownership over the company decides whether, when and how to use the privatisation mandate given by the Parliament. A mandate does not necessarily result in a privatisation.

Source: Submission by the Norwegian authorities.

Professionalised ownership to steer and oversee privatisation

Good practice calls for the privatisation process to be supported, if not administered, by a centralised or coordinated ownership entity which is independent, competent, well-resourced and subject to high standards of accountability and transparency. It should not exercise both regulatory and ownership functions concurrently, as this would present a clear conflict for the privatisation process. Most countries have either vested responsibilities for the privatisation processes in the entities responsible for enterprise ownership, or in the Ministry of Finance (most common in countries with a relatively centralised ownership). Some others have vested the powers in the line ministries that exercise the state's ownership rights.

Where ownership is dispersed among several government bodies, it is imperative to establish a coordinated approach to privatisation. Where cost effective and politically feasible, privatisation should be delegated to a specialised unit (for example in the Ministry of Finance), or to a coordinating body tasked with enhancing collaboration between the government departments involved. This unit would have to be adequately resourced and would ideally report to one clearly identified part of the administration (ideally the executive power), in addition to being subject to the highest standards of transparency and accountability.

In countries with active privatisation programmes, specialised privatisation agencies may be the main players involved in steering the privatisation process, often operating separately from a centralised ownership entity or coordination unit due in part to the sheer volume of transactions. An example can be found in Kazakhstan where the Committee on State Property and Privatisation, a specialised agency established under the Ministry of Finance, is the competent authority for privatisation of state assets, while state ownership is coordinated by a number of state holding companies. Another example is the State Property Fund of Ukraine which is the sole authority authorised to carry out privatisation transactions. Privatisation agencies have become increasingly rare in OECD economies, reflecting the fact that the era of frequent privatisations has come to an end.[3]

Regardless of how privatisation is administered institutionally, the ownership entity or designated privatisation agency or unit plays a central role in seeing through the transaction from beginning to end. It plays a role in the preparation of the SOE for the sale. In anticipation of the sale, it may be involved in modifying the corporate structure, establishing new governance practices, changing management or the board and establishing a "change culture". Where the SOE may have residual liabilities, the ownership unit will decide how to restructure them. The ownership unit will also develop a strategy for the sale. It will manage the relationship with the external advisors (Figure 2.4).

The ownership entity also plays an important role in advising and preparing the government for the transaction. This means working closely with relevant ministers to agree on sale parameters and objectives; valuation; timing of the transaction; ensuring that the appropriate legislative and regulatory frameworks are in place; managing public consultation and securing support from stakeholders; and justifying the privatisation based on an informed decision-making process (see also further below).

In short, the ownership unit is the central actor in managing the privatisation process from start to finish, acting as an intermediary between the SOE, the relevant decision-making bodies, stakeholders, the public and external advisors involved in various stages of the process. It must ensure that the process is balanced with political timetables, economic conditions and market appetite (See Box 2.5 for a case example from the UK).

Figure 2.4. Role of the ownership entity

The ownership entity plays an important role in seeing through the transaction from start to finish.

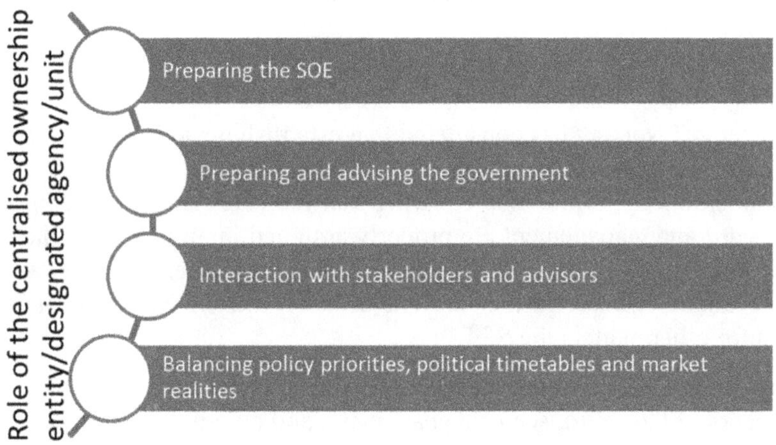

Source: Based on submission from UK authorities.

Box 2.5. UK Government Investments' central role in the privatisation process

UK Government Investments (UKGI) (formerly the Shareholder Executive) is the United Kingdom's centre of excellence for corporate finance and governance across the public sector. While UKGI undertakes a wide variety of activities, it has two main responsibilities: (1) to prepare and execute all significant corporate asset sales by the UK government; and (2) to advise on major corporate finance matters involving the UK's public authorities. The UKGI also represents the UK government as shareholder in relation to a large number of SOEs.

- **In relation to its work on preparing and executing all significant corporate asset sales by the UK Government, UKGI is active across a wide variety of work streams, including:**
  - Making sure SOEs have appropriate and robust commercial strategies in place;
  - Making sure SOEs have the right leadership, management and corporate culture;
  - Putting in place appropriate legal and regulatory structures and governance arrangements; and
  - Where required, restructuring of liabilities.
- **In this work UKGI also plays an important role in readying the UK Government, with its activities including:**
  - Providing advice to ministers and stakeholders across the UK Government on issues including the sales process, valuation, transaction timing and bid assessment;
  - Managing approvals processes within the public sector, including preparing business cases, assessments of value for money and consultations as required;
  - Making sure appropriate legislative and regulatory frameworks are in place ahead of any sale; and
  - Managing the procurement and work of external advisers and, if applicable, also interactions with prospective purchasers during the transaction process.

Source: Submission by UK authorities.

Box 2.6. Establishing a steering group for the transaction: Case example from Norway

Close cooperation with the board and management of the SOE, led by the owner, is vital to the success of the transaction.

The Government of Norway has considered that establishing a steering group when doing IPOs in wholly owned companies has been a key factor in ensuring the privatisation process is run smoothly, while also ensuring that the roles and responsibilities between the owner, board and management are properly assigned in all phases of the process. The steering group does not have specific decision-making powers. Rather, it is set up to coordinate, evaluate and advise the relevant decision maker, which is for some matters the state and for other matters the SOE.

The steering group involves the state-ownership entity normally as "project manager", as well as members of the board, senior management, and external advisor(s).

One of the first tasks of the steering group is to involve the management of the company and its advisors to conduct a "readiness" test. Management then reports back to the steering group as to whether the SOE has all elements in place that can pre-qualify the SOE for a transaction. These elements can include: appropriate corporate governance structures; corporate strategy; reporting and disclosure practices; optimal capital structure, etc.

The steering group will then, together with the board of the company, ensure that the company is/becomes "ready", for example by:

- Defining a proper dividend policy;
- Defining a proper capital structure of the company;
- Clarifying the business strategy and equity story;
- Determining a proper valuation of the company; and/or
- Ensuring the right systems of internal controls are in place.

The "readiness" test will also be key to determine - at the level of the steering group - the timeline for the transaction. The decision to privatise the company might even be postponed should a readiness test reveal that more preparatory work is needed in the company. The steering group plays a key part of an IPO process and ensures that there is a healthy dialogue between the owner and governing bodies, to help the state and the company to make informed decisions and ensure the process is appropriately staged to ensure success.

It should be noted that in the case of a partially state-owned company, especially if it is already stock-exchange listed, the steering group would not include members of the management and board, but only the ownership entity and external advisor. The company would only typically be informed of the planned divestment of state shares immediately before the transaction.

Source: Submission by Norwegian authorities.

Involvement of the SOE board and management: SOEs have an important role in both initiating and implementing their own privatisation. This has been particularly true where the SOEs have enjoyed a large degree of *de facto* autonomy. The government owner often relies on the cooperation of the company, in particular a wholly owned company, in order to ensure that the company is successfully prepared for sale and transition to the private sector, especially when the sale is to be preceded by major restructuring. Getting the company involved as early as possible in the process is key. In Norway, for example, the government establishes a steering group for IPOs of SOEs. This steering group includes two members of the board and top management in the group. As the transaction moves forward, cooperation between steering group members becomes more regular. The company's management plays a key role in assessing the "readiness" of the company for privatisation.

Early stakeholder involvement and communication strategies: Communication and early engagement with stakeholders are cited as key success factors in privatisation (OECD, 2009). The communication campaign should explain the policy objectives of privatisation and the means by which they are to be achieved in order to respond to public concerns and to gain support for the policy. The plan should ensure that public officials from the ownership entity, ministers and company executives have talking points and enough knowledge on the transaction to provide coordinated, coherent and accurate information to the media and public.

Employees of state-owned enterprises constitute a key stakeholder group in the process of privatisation. In this regard, experience from a variety of countries underlines the importance of close involvement of workers and their representatives early and throughout the process. As a first step, information-sharing should take place at an early stage; as a second step, the state as well as the company, through existing institutional arrangements (e.g. tripartite bodies linking governments, employers and trade unions or their equivalent), should engage in more in-depth dialogue and consultation. This dialogue and consultation can inform decision-making and strengthen feasibility of the transaction. Finally, as a third step, when the sale is triggered and if necessitated, the dialogue might transform into a negotiation (collective bargaining) between governments, employers and workers' representatives.

From the point of view of the entity steering the transaction, identification of the issues at the outset, establishment of a consultation timetable, risk mitigation framework and communication plan, and sharing of government plans for mitigating the potential negative effects of privatisation (e.g. on public service delivery, or workers' conditions) helps to dispel any potential employee concerns, and ultimately lead to better privatisation outcomes.

Separately, a communication campaign should be designed to build public support and also share information (as applicable) where public participation may be possible.

Sequencing the process to build credibility and support

One of the important policy decisions for the government is the issue of the order by which assets are privatised and the sequencing of a particular transaction. The experience with decades of privatisation programmes undergone in OECD countries shows that successful programmes usually began with the sale of assets that operate in competitive sectors of the economy and require less preparation. In general, the government will usually begin in sectors where the market structure is already adapted to competition and where the company is ready for sale, in terms of its performance and "readiness".

Another important factor in the sequencing decision is to determine whether the asset will be fully or partially privatised. In some cases, the state may decide to retain majority or partial ownership due to political or strategic imperatives. Some cited examples include where public or national security interests are at stake, for "strategic" reasons, or where the SOEs' sheer size can have systemic impacts. OECD country experience shows that with time, changing political or strategic rationales may also bring about changes to perceptions of necessary partial ownership. One mitigation strategy, if the full privatisation does not garner support, is to break up the SOE into different parts and sell the parts not considered strategic (e.g. the Swedish pharmacy monopoly which was divided into different lots, with some left in state ownership, while others were auctioned off).

In other cases, a partial sale may be necessitated due to following factors: (1) more time is needed for an effective regulatory capacity to develop; (2) staging of the sale can build momentum and gain credibility among investors and the public to facilitate subsequent sales[4]; (3) transactional and market requirements set the pace of sequencing; and (4) the government sees the benefit of maximising proceeds. A selection of national experiences is highlighted in Box 2.7.

Finally, in some cases the sale process may never ultimately take place, which highlights the importance of ensuring the "readiness" of the company before triggering the sell off and being clear of the ownership strategy before embarking on any transaction (see also Chapter 3).

Ultimately, sequencing decisions can build credibility and support for a broader privatisation programme or future privatisation transactions.

Box 2.7. Selected national examples: Sequencing privatisation

Sequencing often takes the form of IPOs, followed by a number of subsequent share offerings. Sequencing is common especially where the privatisation of large or strategic SOEs occurs, but a host of factors can motivate the decision to sequence a privatisation process, as demonstrated by these selected national examples.

- In the United Kingdom, reasons for maintaining a state ownership stake include: (1) benefiting from a potential improvement in performance; (2) ensuring continued involvement in a strategically important activity or for national security reasons; and (3) retaining a degree of influence, including linked to the public interest. Sequencing of privatisation depends also on the wider political landscape and the appetite for the type of corporate assets potentially on offer.
- In France, the maintenance of the state's shares in a company after privatisation is most often based on social, political and strategic motivations. The decision usually accompanies inter-ministerial discussions.
- In Germany, sequencing of privatisation has occurred where particularly large SOEs were being divested. It is deemed that the stock market's capacity to absorb new equities is such that a gradual process is needed to obtain the best price for the state's shares.
- In the Netherlands, the government maintains its ownership in a company if it decides that a public interest needs to be safeguarded through public shareholdings.

Source: OECD (2018).

Notes

[1] It should be noted that the profile of the buyer matters in terms of the impact the change in ownership and management can have on the company. A difference can be seen between the objectives of an industrial buyer versus those of a financial buyer, with the latter most likely involved in a transaction with a shorter-term horizon than an industrial buyer.

[2] OECD (2016a) www.oecd.org/competition/assessment-toolkit.htm.

[3] Where a separate privatisation agency has been set up, the government should not lose its ability to use the appropriate levers it can exercise to affect the pace of privatisation. For example, the privatisation agency may be guided by value maximisation as an overarching policy goal whereas the government has set out a broader set of rationales and objectives to guide the privatisation process. Such goals must be balanced at the outset of the process and should be subject to clear rationales and transparently communicated to the privatisation agency responsible for executing the transaction.

[4] For example, some countries cite the impact of political considerations on the decision to sequence a privatisation, with some parts of the political spectrum being willing to contemplate divestment only if the state remains a dominant owner.

References

OECD (2018), "Privatisation and the Broadening of Ownership of SOEs: Stocktaking of National Practices", https://www.oecd.org/daf/ca/Privatisation-and-the-Broadening-of-Ownership-of-SOEs-Stocktaking-of-National-Practices.pdf.

OECD (2016a), Competition Assessment Toolkit: Principles, www.oecd.org/competition/assessment-toolkit.htm.

OECD (2016b), Broadening the Ownership of State-Owned Enterprises: A Comparison of Governance Practices, http://dx.doi.org/10.1787/9789264244603-en.

OECD (2015), *OECD Guidelines on Corporate Governance of State-Owned Enterprises*, 2015 Edition, http://dx.doi.org/10.1787/9789264244160-en.

OECD (2010), *Privatisation in the 21st Century: Summary of Recent Experiences*, https://www.oecd.org/daf/ca/corporategovernanceofstate-ownedenterprises/43449100.pdf.

OECD (2009), *Privatisation in the 21st Century: Recent Experiences of OECD Countries: Report on Good Practices*, January 2009, https://www.oecd.org/daf/ca/corporategovernanceofstate-ownedenterprises/48476423.pdf.

Chapter 3. Measures to be undertaken before divesting

Prior to privatisation, public authorities will take preparatory steps for the company and possibly for the industry in which the state-owned enterprise operates to prepare for the transaction. This chapter covers: the legal changes required to go from a privatisation candidate to triggering the sell-off; appropriately staging the privatisation process to ensure success; pre-privatisation industry/company restructuring; addressing employee and stakeholder relations and concerns; deciding on the appropriate method of sale; and ensuring effective communication, transparency and integrity of the process.

Prior to privatisation, public authorities will take preparatory steps for the company and possibly for the industry in which the state-owned enterprise (SOE) operates to prepare for the transaction. This chapter covers the following areas: the legal changes required to go from a privatisation candidate to triggering the sell-off; appropriately staging the privatisation process to ensure success; pre-privatisation industry/company restructuring; addressing employee and stakeholder relations and concerns; deciding on the appropriate method of sale; and ensuring effective communication, transparency and integrity of the process.

Going from privatisation candidate to triggering the sell-off

To go from a privatisation candidate to triggering the sell-off, a number of legal changes will need to take place to formalise the sell-off. In many cases, this will include legal acts by parliament (e.g. the repeal, amendment and/or enactment of laws); sell mandates to government; new sector legislation; or revising specific SOE legislation (for example related to public policy objectives). The approach to legislation is largely a reflection of the existing legal framework, the way the SOEs are organised and the size and scope of the privatisation activity foreseen.

In general, two broad approaches to privatisation-specific legislation can be distinguished.

- *Framework legislation*: Some countries, especially those that still have ongoing privatisation programmes, have one unifying privatisation law, or a mosaic of laws bearing on privatisation processes. Under this approach, a comprehensive framework is put in place to address all aspects of the privatisation process, from the institutional and decision-making organisation to the disposal of the asset. The purpose of such legislation is to state the objectives of privatisation and the principles governing it, and to specify the institutional structure. In some cases, the legislation also seeks to provide for modalities of privatisation and to create special rights for the state post-sale, or conditions for the sale of shares to employees. Finally, a framework law usually contains a broad delegation of powers to the administration to deal with privatisation particularities. Typically, countries where the scale and scope of the privatisation activity has been large have adopted this approach because it provides the government with greater flexibility and predictability to formulate and implement privatisation policies.
- *Transaction-based legislation:* More infrequent privatisers generally have no overarching law for a privatisation programme, but in many cases pass a privatisation bill for each transaction, if this is required. A variation of the latter approach is employed in Japan, where legal authorisation is needed for privatisation, but can be combined with other legislative acts. Finally, some countries apply a more "public finance approach" according to which the conversion of corporate assets into financial assets is mostly a question of value-for-money, which does not require legal measures.

Whether or not parliamentary approval is needed varies across jurisdictions and may vary according to the level of ownership and control that is relinquished. For example, in Finland, under the State Shareholders and Ownership Steering Act, all decisions identifying the companies in which the state may relinquish its sole ownership (100% of the votes) or its control (minimum of 50.1% of the votes) of a given company are to be made by parliament. All other decisions on the sales of shares are made by the government.

It should be noted that some jurisdictions have taken additional steps to simplify privatisation procedures to avoid having to seek parliamentary approval for transaction-based privatisation depending on the nature of the transaction. This has helped to depoliticise the decision-making around privatisation as well as speed-up transactions when there is sufficient rationale, transparency and consensus around the government's privatisation priorities.

Box 3.1. Simplifying privatisation procedures: Case example from France

In France recent changes to the privatisation regime have simplified privatisation procedures where a decree or ministerial approval is sufficient to pursue the transaction. The criteria for simplified procedures are often based on the level of ownership and control that is relinquished. The table below summarises the legal instrument(s) required based on the type of privatisation operation. As a general rule of thumb, where the privatisation involves the transfer of a majority of the company's share capital, a large SOE (in terms of employment or turnover), or a company that has been under state ownership for over five years, a legal act and decree are required. For most other transactions, a ministerial decree is sufficient.

Operation	Legal instrument
Transfer of the majority of a company's share capital to the private sector following sale by the government of shareholdings* in a company	Act + decree
Transfer of the majority of a company's share capital to the private sector in which it owned a majority stake for over five years with staff > 500 or turnover > €75m**	Act + decree
Transfer of the majority of a company's share capital to the private sector with an air- or road-transport infrastructure as part of a concession awarded by the government and LFB Group	Act + decree
Transfer of the majority of a company's share capital to the private sector (other than those cases covered above)	Decree
Transfer of the majority of a company's share capital to the private sector following sale by a public entity, government-owned company or Caisse des Dépôts et Consignations (CDC) of a stake in a company with staff > 1 000 or turnover > €150m **	Prior authorisation by the Minister of Economy
Transfer of the majority of a company's share capital to the private sector following sale by a local or regional authority of a stake in a company with staff > 500 or turnover > €75m**	Decision by the local or regional authority's decision-making body
Sale of a government shareholding which results in it being less than one or two-thirds of the share capital	Decree
Other sales by the government	Decree by the Minister of Economy
Other sales by a public entity, publicly-owned company or the CDC	*Not subject to legislation*

* Shareholding applies to any portion of share capital owned (Art. 2 I Paragraph 1)
**Including subsidiaries in which a majority stake is held either directly or indirectly
NB: Sales include operations that produce the same result (including capital increases leading to a dilution in the government's shareholding) (Art. 22 V c)
Source: Commission des Participations et des Transferts (2016).

At the same time, it should be recognised that embedding privatisation in the legislative process could have important beneficial impacts on the transparency and predictability of the process. Even governments that are formally entitled to privatise state assets without specific legal authorisation, or that need only to seek the "approval" of parliament, have sometimes chosen to pass a sales act setting out the agreed modalities of privatisation (see

Box 3.1). This has ensured that the privatisation process has secured legitimacy and agreement of stakeholders prior to embarking on the process.

Most countries have other specific rules applying to privatisation, for example provisions contained in public procurement rules, securities laws (in the case of public offerings) or general company law, which may naturally have ramifications for privatisation. However, these are not discussed in this section.

Appropriately staging the privatisation process

One of the key decisions facing privatisation officials relates to the staging of sales, in other words for how much and how fast the company should be sold. The decision as to whether the enterprise is to be sold in stages, or all at once, and how quickly is influenced by the interplay of the following factors: (a) company-related factors; (b) transaction-related factors such as the size of the asset and the absorptive capacity of the market; and (c) market structure and the existence of an adequate regulatory capacity.

Company-related factors - "Readiness"

Traditionally, many OECD governments have approached privatisation by starting with partial privatisation in order to increase total proceeds. Under this approach the state-owned enterprise is given an opportunity to improve its performance, build a track record in the market (particularly if investors are unfamiliar with the sector), overcome the price discounting arising from information asymmetries and fetch a higher price for the subsequent tranches. Furthermore, by retaining a stake in the company, the government can signal its confidence in the future of the company and its interest in maximising the value of its shareholding.

However, the success of this strategy is closely linked to government credibility in the market (see also Chapter 5 on good governance practices in cases of partial privatisation). If the partially privatised asset is vulnerable to government interference, this creates uncertainty for investors with adverse effects on the value of shares. It also means that the full benefits of privatisation in terms of improved efficiency may not be realised. It also does not result in full risk transfer to the private sector and could expose the government to moral hazard where the company is too big or important to fail. Nowadays, with less SOEs being listed in stock markets across the OECD area, sales strategies have shifted toward direct sales as the preferred sales methods.

One of the key questions the owner should determine is the "readiness" of the SOE to be privatised and that will depend on the company and its qualities. In Norway, the government systematically involves the board and management of wholly owned SOEs, through a steering group, to enlist their support before embarking on the privatisation process. The company's management is asked to conduct a "readiness review", which will evaluate whether the company has the appropriate corporate governance structures; strategy; reporting and disclosure practices; as well as capital structure. All these factors will be key to ensure the company's value is increased should the privatisation transaction ensue; it may also lead to terminating the sales process should the owner determine the company is not "ready". Some of the key areas to focus on include:

- *Corporate governance:* Does the company adhere to high standards of corporate governance, including the relevant code of corporate governance, or listing requirements?

- *Strategy:* Have the board and management streamlined the company? This may differ depending on the transaction mode selected (i.e. IPO, M&A, partial or full privatisation). The company will need to focus on identifying the main value drivers. For each transaction these will differ and the strategy must be "tailor made". Moreover, much of the strategy pursued will depend on the sector in which it operates.
- *Capital structure:* The owner and board will need to deal with putting in place an optimal capital structure for the company. This might include defining a clear strategy and targets or adapting the state's rate-of-return requirements and dividend policy.
- *Non-commercial objectives:* If the company is carrying out non-commercial objectives (e.g. public policy objectives, public service obligations, or an industrial strategy), the state will need to determine what will become of those objectives and how they will continue to be fulfilled (if relevant) following the transaction.

Based on the company's "readiness", the owner must then devise its own strategy for the transaction. This means being clear on: its own objectives and the level of ownership it may or may not wish to retain in the company; if it retains shares, what its strategy will be for the remaining shares it owns; the level of commercial/non-commercial objectives the company will retain, etc. Once "readiness" has been established, other factors will be important to determine whether the sale will go through including investor appetite and market conditions.

Transaction-related factors

Transaction-related factors such as the size of the asset and the absorptive capacity of the market also matter. In some cases the gradual approach to privatisation is dictated by the sheer size of the entity (too big to be sold in its entirety) and the limited absorptive capacity of the market, requiring that the sale be carried out in instalments.

Market-related factors

The market structure also matters. This means ensuring that the privatisation occurs in a context where there is adequate regulatory capacity to address potential concerns of excessive market power. A partial privatisation is often used as an interim step, even if the longer-term goal is full divestiture, to provide sufficient time for the development of the desired market structure along with the institutions that are necessary for the successful operation of the company.

Pre-privatisation industry restructuring

The consensus position among OECD countries is that a government should not privatise an SOE before an appropriate regulatory framework for the privatised entity has been established (it should be noted that this point is moot if those changes have already taken place well before the privatisation transaction). This implies that a privatising government needs to ensure that two separate, but related, regulatory frameworks are in place. First, an adequate competition or anti-trust regulation backed by effective enforcement mechanisms is needed. The consensus view is that privatised entities involved in any activity where competition on general market terms is feasible should be made subject to competitive pressures. This can be determined through a competition assessment (See OECD, 2009).

Box 3.2. Good practices in pre-privatisation industry restructuring

OECD, 2009 identified good practices with regard to pre-privatisation industry restructuring that can be summarised as follows:

- Governments should normally not privatise SOEs before an appropriate regulatory framework has been established. This framework includes anti-trust regulation to ensure competition where feasible and specialised regulation to oversee activities where an element of monopoly is likely to persist.
- Existing laws and regulations (including anti-trust and takeover rules) should apply to the privatisation itself. If exemptions are granted, such exemptions would need to be justified and fully disclosed in advance.
- The regulatory functions whose domain will be affected by privatisation need to be separated from the privatising unit, the state's ownership unit and the executive powers. This can be obtained through the creation of an autonomous regulatory body outside the control of the executive powers or through, at least, a complete functional and legal separation within the state.
- Good practice calls for exposing as much as possible of an SOE's activities to competition no later than at the time of privatisation. If monopoly activities necessarily remain the government faces a choice:
    - Break up the company, sell the competitive parts and make specific regulatory arrangements for the rest;
    - If the company is to remain vertically integrated during and after privatisation then there is a heightened need for independent and well-resourced regulation.

Source: From OECD, 2009.

This leaves a residual role for the second important regulatory framework, namely sectoral regulation (for instance, third party access regulation) of activities that will necessarily involve an element of monopoly subsequent to privatisation. A further consequence of the consensus is that safeguards must be taken to ensure the independence of the relevant regulatory agencies in general and *vis-à-vis* any remaining ownership function that the government may retain. This underlines the primordial recommendation promoted by the *OECD Guidelines on Corporate Governance of State-Owned Enterprises* ("OECD SOE Guidelines") to separate ownership and regulatory functions (OECD, 2009).

An additional issue is the degree to which the SOE considered for privatisation – or parts of it – can be subjected to competition. In the network industries, this is referred to as "structural separation". SOEs in the network industries generally consist of many parts, some of which will remain monopolies. Through the process of structural separation, the latter parts are separated from those that are capable of operating in a competitive environment. In some past experiences where governments have privatised vertically integrated SOEs and introduced competition later, this has not been an effective strategy to achieve the long term goal of maximising economic efficiency through privatisation, as it simply creates a privatised monopoly with the potential for the monopoly to abuse its position (OECD, 2009).

In most cases, the government has opted to separate "commercial" parts of a utility, typically including the retail side of business, as part of the corporatisation process. What then happens depends on national preferences. These units may be privatised subject to standard competition policy safeguards, or they may be retained as independent subsidiaries of the SOE whilst their competition with private entities is introduced.

Box 3.3. Restructuring and privatisation in the EU: State Aid considerations

The European Commission's Guidance Paper on state aid-compliant financing, restructuring and privatisation of state-owned enterprises helps to clarify instances of state aid when undergoing a privatisation process.

The EU has developed guidance clarifying the impact that state aid rules could have on the policies and decisions of member states undergoing economic adjustment programmes, which have committed to reducing the strain on public finances among others by restructuring and/or privatising SOEs.

For privatisations not to entail state aid, public authorities must ensure that they are done on market terms and that no advantage (typically in the form of foregone revenues) is given to the buyer and/or the sold undertaking. This is particularly the case for highly indebted companies, for which liquidation is a plausible option.

In order to identify or exclude the presence of state aid in the privatisation context, the Commission relies on the Market Economy Vendor Principle (MEVP), i.e. the assumption that a private vendor that intends to sell his company would do so for the highest possible price and without imposing conditions that would be liable to depress the price. When selling (assets of) a publicly-owned company, the member state – in order to exclude the presence of state aid – must in principle likewise behave as a market economy vendor seeking to maximise the revenues (or minimise the loss) from the sale.

In order to make the company more interesting for potential buyers, member states may decide to "clean" or restructure the asset side and/or liability side of the company's balance sheet. These preparatory measures for the privatisation of SOE will in many instances entail state aid, possibly in the form of restructuring aid or as pure financial measures without any accompanying changes to the firm's business or corporate governance model.

In particular, write-off of state debt, debt-to-equity/asset conversion and capital increases before privatisation will constitute state aid if they do not adhere to the principles explained above. Conversely, in the case of privatisation by IPO or sale of shares on the stock exchange, debt may be written off or reduced without this giving rise to state aid in the specific case where the proceeds of the flotation exceed the reduction in debt.

Source: European Commission (2012).

The final choice is whether the hard core monopoly elements of utilities SOEs should themselves be privatised. The retention of such "natural monopolies" under public control is widely supported by economic theory and in practice the main argument for transferring them to private ownership is normally a need to address major operational inefficiencies that have accumulated due to the public ownership. Privatising such enterprises highlights the need for independent and well-resourced regulation. A case in point is the so-called universal service obligations (USOs) that will normally follow this part of the enterprise. A means of treating USOs post privatisation will need to be established. If the SOE is corporatised, and perhaps sequentially privatised, then public service obligations are identified, costs funded and, ultimately, a contractual process is made to ensure fulfilment of those obligations to ensure competitive neutrality (OECD, 2012). In the case of a vertically integrated privatisation the state can impose USOs on buyers and let the competitive sale process sort the costing and funding out, however as mentioned this is not a preferred route (OECD, 2009).

Regardless of the restructuring option, special attention will need to be paid to the competitive conditions that it creates for potential or actual competitors on the market; and for the ultimate outcome to ensure competitive neutrality. In the case of the EU and European Economic Area countries, this is particularly important to ensure that any eventual restructuring does not result in violations of EU State Aid rules (see Box 3.3). A case study from the Latvian banking sector is an example of such pre-privatisation restructuring necessitated by EU State Aid rules (Box 3.3).

Box 3.4. Restructuring before privatisation: Case example from Latvia

Sale of Citadele Bank

Parex Bank – the second largest bank in Latvia in terms of total assets (~EUR 5 billion at the time) – was severely hit by the financial crisis in 2008. The Republic of Latvia regarded the bank as being of systemic importance for the financial system, hence provided substantial state aid, including capital aid, liquidity aid and state guarantees. Given its extensive restructuring and banking experience the European Bank for Reconstruction and Development (EBRD) became a shareholder in Parex Bank (25% plus one share) in 2009. This immediately sent a strong positive signal to the clients of the bank and strengthened the bank's viability.

As the European Commission has strict rules on exceptional cases in which governments can provide support to commercial entities, Latvia and Parex Bank undertook extensive commitments restricting the use of state aid in view of a complete disposal of state ownership within a strict timeframe.

In 2010, as per a restructuring plan approved by the European Commission, Parex Bank was split into a so-called "good bank" taking over all core assets (Citadele Bank) and a so-called "bad bank", which kept the remaining non-core and non-performing assets (Reverta). Specific behavioural and disposal commitments remained in force for each institution.

In December 2013, the Latvian government approved a strategy for finding investors for Citadele Bank. A high-level Steering Committee comprising various stakeholders (relevant ministries, the EBRD, Citadele Bank) was set up to drive and supervise the sales process. At the outset a number of financial and non-financial (policy) objectives were defined and thereafter approved by the Latvian government including, *inter alia*, stability of the financial system, diversification of local banking capital sources, development of the local stock market, achieving the highest possible value and full compliance with EU state aid regulations.

Following an international tender, Société Générale and Linklaters were appointed as the investment bank and the legal advisor, respectively, to organise the sales process in line with best practices. Following a 12-month dual track (M&A and IPO) sales process, at the end of 2014 a group of highly reputable international investors led by the US investment firm Ripplewood acquired a majority stake in Citadele Bank. The EBRD retained its shareholding. The bank is still owned by the same shareholder group. The sale of Citadele Bank to private investors has fostered further development of the bank and benefited the Latvian financial sector.

Owing to the scale of the transaction and the considerable public funds involved, the sale of Citadele Bank attracted strong media attention and triggered public debate. A number of ex-post audits have been conducted to date (for example by the State Audit Office and the Parliamentary Investigation Commission) to evaluate the results of the sales transaction. Several key observations and conclusions can be drawn from the sales transaction itself and the results of the ex-post evaluations:

- Non-financial (policy) objectives are usually not communicated or explained sufficiently to the general public.
- The achievement of non-financial (policy) objectives is more difficult to measure and their impact is usually visible in the medium term, hence many ex-post reviews tend to focus excessively on evaluating only financial outcomes. Ex-post evaluations also tend to take into account information not available at the time of the actual transaction ("in hindsight").
- Balancing strict confidentiality requirements usually applicable to M&A and IPO transactions with the need for high transparency in transactions connected with disposing assets directly or indirectly owned by the state has proven to be a challenge for all stakeholders involved.

Source: Submission from the Latvian authorities.

Pre-privatisation company restructuring, legal changes and other factors

Pre-privatisation restructuring is not a pre-requisite for all transactions, and is best handled on a case-by-case basis. The degree and need for company-specific restructuring is shaped by factors such as: the size of the enterprise; the planned method of sale; the structure of the market in which it operates; government objectives with respect to the envisaged market structure post-privatisation; and environmental impacts.

Typically, privatisation of larger companies and of those operating in monopoly sectors of the economy are preceded by company-specific restructuring. This process may or may not be part of broader changes as markets are liberalised and competition is introduced.

Pre-privatisation restructuring of SOEs is more commonplace prior to IPOs. However, in some cases restructuring may help attract more bidders to a trade sale auction and hence boost the proceeds. As discussed in previous sections, the market structure and the government's objectives concerning the introduction of competition are other significant determinants of restructuring decisions.

Figure 3.1. Pre-privatisation company restructuring, legal changes and other factors

Where restructuring occurs, it can pertain to (see also Figure 3.1):

1. *Strategic restructuring whereby the corporate performance, business strategy and focus of the company are considered.* This might include making changes to board composition; and if the board so decides, making changes to the management composition to make a shift in management culture or putting in place new leadership with the right skills and a strong commitment to privatisation. It might also pertain to improving corporate governance practices and possibly bringing them in line with existing corporate governance codes and listing requirements, or revisiting the business plan or corporate strategy of the company. It might also involve ensuring the company is subject to certain levels of transparency and disclosure and has appropriate control systems in place on par with private sector peers.
2. *Operational restructuring pertaining to management or at the employment level.* Where countries have strict employment protection laws or special employment regimes for public employees, restructuring may pertain to public sector employee contracts or the restructuring of pension liabilities. It may pertain to the issue of remuneration and the use of options in compensating company leadership, including share ownership.
3. *Financial restructuring.* This may include restructuring of the corporate balance sheet to align the debt-equity ratio with the prevailing levels in the private sector. It might pertain to restructuring of liabilities, ensuring a sustainable and optimal capital structure and the general "cleaning up" of the company balance sheet in order to make it marketable and to increase its potential value. The state owner might also re-evaluate its rate-of-return requirements and dividend policy in view of a potential privatisation.
4. *Legal and regulatory restructuring.* Changes to the legal form of the company may be necessitated to adapt to the regulatory requirements in the market place. This might relate to separating monopoly elements or "strategic" activities from SOEs prior to privatisation - this is often seen in the public utilities sector. There may also be a need to divest SOEs of certain assets prior to privatisation. This question has for example arisen: when the company had subsidiaries that were either incongruent with its own business plans and hence could complicate

privatisation; when the subsidiaries were held jointly with enterprises other than the potential purchasers; and when the combined market share of the subsidiaries and the potential purchasers gave rise to antitrust concerns. In other cases this might pertain to separating assets of relevance to national security.

5. *Ownership restructuring.* In countries with active privatisation programmes, a decision may be required to shift the exercise of ownership rights from one entity (e.g. line ministry) to an entity assigned by law to carry out the transaction (e.g. privatisation agency). Careful design of the process, including support from the highest level is necessary to ensure smooth transfer subject to agreed timelines.

Other factors to take into consideration during this phase include undertaking due diligence required prior the privatisation and specific risk mitigation plans to deal with them. Due diligence can cover all aspects of the transaction, including potentially environmental audit in case of residual environmental liabilities (Box 3.5).

This category also covers the separation of non-national security related assets which will not be slated for privatisation - for example non-corporatised assets such as real estate, or items of art or of public interest which would be potentially separated out prior to the privatisation.

Box 3.5. Dealing with environmental liabilities

SOEs that are subject to standard environmental rules may (like any other company) carry heavy environmental liabilities due to polluting activities in the past. National privatisation practices in respect of these appear to differ, with a majority of countries transferring these liabilities to the privatised entities, but a few (e.g. Austria, Slovak Republic and Sweden) under some circumstances either assuming the responsibility or compensating buyers accordingly. The national differences may reflect privatisation methods. In the case of the trade sale of an entire SOE, environmental liabilities would be the subject of buyer and seller due diligence and reflected in the ultimate sale price. Where SOEs are offered through IPOs to the public it may be politically less easy for governments to "wash their hands" of longstanding environmental liabilities. However, in that case they need to ensure themselves that any compensation paid to the SOE in this regard does not rise to the level of unintended (or, in the case of EU countries, illegal) state aid.

Source: OECD (2009).

Addressing employee and stakeholder relationships and concerns

As mentioned earlier, involvement and consultation with employees and labour representation early in the process is critical to ensure its success. Before undertaking a divestment, the state owner should be informed of the applicable labour laws and civil service codes and their impact on the treatment of SOE employees during and after the privatisation process. This varies significantly across countries. For example, in some North European and other countries civil service status cannot be rescinded, so if the employees of an SOE prior to privatisation have civil servant contracts then these contracts must either be grandfathered post privatisation or the individuals must be offered alternative employment. In other countries the SOE employees' contractual situation and salaries are adapted to the conditions in the private sector, but they are offered mitigation measures such as direct financial compensation or employee shares.

In some countries job security is offered to the SOE employees of privatisation candidates. This can take the form of either employment retention guarantees as part of the state's agreement with the buyer, or post privatisation controls. Such measures may be either generally offered or, more commonly, the state may have the option of applying them. Some examples are provided in Box 3.6.

Box 3.6. Treatment of SOE employees during and after privatisation: national practices

Most countries do not report specific measures for the treatment of employees during and after privatisation. For those that do, a sample of national practices is provided below.

- In Turkey, the Privatisation Law establishes a number of compensation and mitigation schemes available to SOE employees that lose their jobs due to privatisation. These include a special "job loss compensation" in addition to the redundancy payment rules generally in force; rules on the reassignment of redundant staff within the affected organisation or among public institutions; social assistance supplements to eligible individuals; and pension bonuses to staff qualifying for early retirement.
- In the United Kingdom, if the status of employees changes as a result of the restructuring of the business, it is possible that for incumbent staff certain terms and conditions apply to protect employees' rights. This pertains to the Terms and Conditions under the Transfer of Undertakings (Protection of Employment) [TUPE] Regulations 2006 (updated by new Regulations in 2014) which applies to organisations of all sizes and protects employees' rights when an organisation they work for transfers to a new employer. The TUPE applies when employees are moving from government employment to private sector employment.
- In France, the legal framework applicable to privatisation does not include any special provisions for the treatment of affected workers. This treatment is subject to the common law of companies and to labour law (in particular where there is a transfer of an undertaking), or public employees may be the subject of discussions between the state and the acquirer of the public shareholdings in question. However, in certain procedures for the sale of securities, the state may wish, before the transfer, that the purchaser define a social project in the offer, including information on changes in employment in the company. Thus, in the specifications published by the state concerning the privatisations of the airport companies of Lyon and Nice, the state asked the purchasing candidates to present proposals on wage policy, profit-sharing and employee participation.
- In Germany, there is no general provision. Insofar as members of staff are civil servants benefitting from interminable appointment, their contractual entitlements must be respected and preserved. Provisions on the employment of civil servants post privatisation would require specific legal action. Examples in the past have included the transfer of civil servants to SOEs not slated for privatisation.

Source: OECD (2018).

Should a significant restructuring process be accompanied by a workforce reduction before or anticipated immediately following the sale, it is important to involve employee representatives at the enterprise level to discuss, anticipate and mitigate effects on employment and the company. Although this consultation happens at the enterprise level, the entity responsible for steering the transaction should ensure that the appropriate structures are in place to ensure meaningful information exchange, consultation and negotiation.

Separately, and as discussed in later sections of this report, some jurisdictions may incorporate special provisions (in terms of pricing; number of shares for "Minimum Lot"; preferred bonus share) for employees to participate in the privatisation process itself, specifically in the case of a public offering. In Italy's recent IPOs involving SOEs (e.g. Italian Postal Services Group), a "special" tranche was addressed to employees residing in Italy to participate also in the retail Italian tranche of the offering reserved for domestic retail buyers. The orders were submitted to the intermediaries for a minimum number of shares (the "Minimum Lot for Employees") or multiples thereof. The so-called Minimum Lot is lower than the ordinary one (for instance, 50 shares for the employees versus 500 shares for the retail investors) and the employees may have different bonus shares after a defined holding period (1:10 for the employees versus 1:20 for other retail investors).

Deciding on the appropriate method of sale

This section explores the merits and demerits of different privatisation methods, including their possible impact on privatisation proceeds, the market and corporate performance.

The choice of privatisation methods is guided, among other factors, by the size of the enterprises to be sold, market conditions and the objectives of the process. It should be noted that often the government will not have a menu of options to determine the sales method, as this will depend on the business and the government's objectives, as well as the asset, market conditions and other external factors. The sales method and timing of the transaction may also change, or in some more extreme cases may be terminated mid-way through the process if the owner determines that its objectives and rationales (which will vary from transaction to transaction) set at the start of the process are not met.

Among countries, privatisation methods may also vary according to the relative maturity of the economy in which the privatisation is taking place. The post-transition economies have mostly sold off small SOEs through trade-sale auctions to strategic private investors. Most other countries have relied on share offerings to privatise large companies and trade sales to privatise smaller firms. Privatisation through management buy-outs has become rare, but it still occurs. The main privatisation methods, described in further detail in the sub-sections below, are as follows (Table 3.1):

- public share offerings in the stock market (see also special section below)
- trade sales/auction to private firms
- management and employee buy-outs
- a combination of more than one of the above methods.

It should also be noted that the ownership entity will have a varying degree of involvement in "steering" the privatisation transaction depending on the method of sale chosen. For example, for a merger and acquisition, the owner will typically be very involved in that process because it involves selling its shares. If divestment entails a public share offering, this process would typically involve the board and management, which would be selling the company on behalf of the owner. The level of advisory services will also be adjusted depending on the method of sale.

Table 3.1. Typology of privatisation methods

Method	Form	Description	Merits	Demerits
Trade sale/auction	Private sale	a) Negotiated sale: Sell a portion of SOE to a preferred private bidder; b) Block trades: Offering tranches of shares in already listed SOEs privately to groups of investors	-Strategic investor -Suitable for SMEs -Introduces management changes and technology infusion -Less restructuring required -Cheaper and faster than IPO	- No revenue maximisation - No need to adhere to stringent listing requirements - Lack of process integrity - Not suitable for very large companies - Not suitable if concerns about competition
	Trade sale auctions	Auctioning off a portion or all to highest bidder	Best price	Potential discounts especially if not restructured
Share offerings	Initial public offering (IPO)	Offering a tranche of shares on the stock exchange(s)	-Good governance and management practices -Potential for good performance	-Dispersed shareholding -Expensive to execute -Pricing and valuation tricky
	Secondary public offering (SPO)	Offering additional tranches of SOE shares following IPO	-Raises capital for seller and company	-No choice in strategic investor
	Accelerated book building (a form of SPO)	Placing tranches of shares of already listed SOEs with institutional investors	- Less expensive and speedier	-Prices come at a discount to public offering
	Convertible bonds	Disposing of additional tranches of listed SOEs through the issuing of convertible bonds	- Credibility enhancing for privatisation programme -Adaptable to market realities	- Postpones transfer of ownership - Investor decides on convertibility - Not commonly used
	Privatisation by SOE	Issuing additional stock to dilute ownership share	-Need to shore up capital base	
Management/ employee buy-out	Trade sale	Shares sold to legal entities controlled by staff and/or management	- Suitable for smaller companies - Garners support for privatisation programme - Aligns incentives	- Conflicting objectives - Corporate governance weaknesses - Forgo value

Note: Secondary public offerings are generally not included in the scope of this Guide.
Source: Drawing on OECD (2003), OECD (2009) and Author.

Public share offering

What is it?

Privatisation through public share offerings is an open competitive process whereby the shares of a company are floated on the stock market. Initial public offerings (IPOs) are the most transparent method of sale, but are also the most expensive approach due to the complexity of the process which also often requires more specialised expertise than for example trade sales, raising the likelihood that governments will need to draw on external advice. They require a great deal of preparation and planning, involve significant restructuring of the company, and draw heavily on the services of a vast array of advisors. These include lawyers, accountants, investment bankers, industry consultants, public relations professionals and marketing advisors. In addition to transferring ownership and raising funds for the selling shareholder (i.e. the government), public offers often raise additional capital for an enterprise through the issue of new shares and this capital can be used to grow the business, repay external debt, etc. (see Figure 3.2 and Special Section).

Depending on the size of the offering and the depth of the domestic capital markets, investors targeted for such IPOs could originate from the domestic market and/or international markets. Moreover, the listing itself could originate in the domestic stock market or abroad.

When is it most appropriate?

An IPO requires the enterprise being privatised to be of sufficient size and quality to justify a public sale of shares. Given the amount of preparation and the costs involved, public share offerings have typically been used to privatise larger companies with a potential for good performance and where there is sufficient market appetite. The company will also need to have governance and management practices that can sustain the scrutiny of investors and capital markets regulators. This means, for example, being able to comply with listing requirements[1] and national corporate governance codes, reinforcing independent directors in decision-making and other such features which provide confidence and protection to investors and ultimately lead to a more transparent and efficient management.

Privatisation through share offering requires the existence of a relatively well-developed financial and legal infrastructure. This means stock markets that are relatively liquid and deep and a fairly sophisticated set of laws governing property rights, companies, insolvency and bankruptcy. In some cases, privatisation has in itself served as a vehicle for enlarging and deepening local capital markets.

Disadvantages?

Public offerings tend to produce dispersed shareholdings which in the absence of a well-functioning market for corporate control can deprive the company of strong governance. In terms of the revenues raised, public offerings are generally more expensive to execute compared to a trade sale due to the complexity of the transaction and reliance on specialised expertise, and could entail some degree of loss of revenue arising from discounting of shares and offering incentives.[2] Moreover, IPOs/secondary sales are often more expensive than other sales because of the fee structure of underwriting banks which take on risk on behalf of the seller (see also Box 3.5).

Furthermore, public share offerings lack the degree of flexibility afforded by other forms of privatisation. For example, privatisation through a public share offering does not necessarily bring in expertise and experience from a specific strategic investor, who could for example introduce more efficient management methods, introduce new technology and know-how, enhance profitability, etc. For this reason, company restructuring may be necessary before undertaking the public offering process.

How does it work?

In the course of the IPO, shares are usually offered to retail and institutional investors, although this process is decided by the government, the company and the managers of the share issue on a case-by-case basis. In the case of share issue privatisations, most are fixed-price methods where the government decides on a share price a few weeks in advance of the offering date. Governments typically use tender offers or book-building for the institutional or foreign tranches. A fixed price method is popular with risk averse issuers; whereas governments may be more willing to use book building or auctions to maximise issue proceeds in subsequent offerings (Jones *et al.*, 1999; OECD, 2016). In other cases, for example in Sweden, share price intervals are quite common with a ceiling. The interval can range between 5 and 6, and up to a 20 % difference between the lowest and highest offer price. Depending on the share demand the final offer price can be higher or lower. This is quite common for companies that are difficult to value prior to going public.

Secondary offering is the public offering of shares of an already listed company. It is used for example when companies are of such a substantial size that a sale of the targeted percentage to investors could not be made in a single transaction, or, more often, when governments want to further reduce their stake in a company following an IPO. The sales process may be less complex than that of the IPO; for example, setting a price for shares may be less difficult because the shares are already traded and have a market price.

Another form of secondary offering is through the process of accelerated book building (ABB) the government charges a number of financial intermediaries (typically investment banks) with placing tranches of shares of already listed SOEs with institutional investors. ABB is a technique mainly used for divestments of shares to institutional investors, which reduces preparation periods (less than a month) and execution window (a few days), allowing to minimise legal and other related costs. It does not require the presentation of a prospectus nor the creation of advertising campaigns. As such it can allow for flexibility and differentiated market exposure according to various implementation methods. The prices obtained may come at a discount relative to public offerings, but this is compensated for by the relative cheapness and speediness of the method (Box 3.7).

A separate form of share offering of a rarer nature involves capital increases by SOEs themselves. Such transactions are usually motivated by a perception that capital cover of the enterprise has become too thin and that there is an unwillingness – especially in the case of partly owned SOEs – on the part of the government to contribute fresh capital. Capital increases are also seen in combination with share offerings by the government itself, a method that may in practice be a close substitute to adjusting the capital structure of the SOE prior to privatisation (OECD, 2009).

Box 3.7. Accelerated book building sale: Case example from Italy

In October 2014, the Italian Ministry of Economy and Finance announced its intention to sell a minority stake in the national electricity company (ENEL), to be carried out with the use of sale techniques suitable for a quick equity placement aimed, directly or indirectly, at institutional investors. Similar procedures were already used in the past and the Ministry was supported by a financial advisor - acting also as independent appraiser - and by a primary international law firm for what concerned the legal aspects of the deal. The sale of the fifth tranche of ENEL was carried out using a process of an Accelerated Book Building (ABB) with a backstop clause.

The ABB is considered a favoured technique due to minimised costs, maximum flexibility and quick execution period. In the case of ENEL the transaction was preceded by the identification of 14 banks which presented their price offers at the start of the transaction. The bids were for a fixed purchase and then were followed by a placement (on the market or with investors' institutions) of a substantial quantity of the offered stake.

According to the Italian authorities, the backstop clause ensures a minimum level of the sale price and transfers risk for unsold amounts to the bank syndicate. In other words, the backstop assures that a defined amount of shares will be purchased even if there are not enough interested investors. By entering into a strong commitment of underwriting, the banks have full responsibility for the quantity of shares guaranteed, if they initially go unsold, and provide the necessary funds in exchange for the available shares.

Starting from October 2014, the Ministry of Economy and Finance has monitored the equity markets and the performance of the ENEL stock, in order to identify the most appropriate time window for the potential placement of 540 116 400 shares, equal to 5.74% of the entire share capital. On 25th of February 2015, due to the positive intra-daily performance of the security, the Ministry started the sale process, inviting the previously selected banks to present their bids.

Four banks offered the best backstop price, which involved a 1.2% discount compared to the closing price of the previous days and as such were selected as joint book runners. The deal yielded an overall income of around EUR 2.2 billion, used in the same year for buying back Italian Government Securities.

The price on the official market showed a slight reduction the day after the ABB, mainly due to technical reasons in the allocation process of the shares by the banks. However, in the following days, ENEL shares reached the maximum range of price in the period of last three years, which has been cited as a factor of success and "fair market value" sale by the Italian authorities.

Source: Submission from the Italian authorities

Trade sale/auction

What is it?

A trade sale involves the direct sale of shares of a state-owned enterprise or asset from the government to the buyer through negotiations or a process based on competitive bidding. In many cases, the buyer can be a strategic investor which has the same operations and its acquisition of that stake is in line with their overall expansion strategy. However, increasingly, private equity firms have also figured among buyers - especially prior to the global financial and economic crisis. The percentage acquired is often 100% of the company. In some cases, however, it can represent a minority stake in a privatised entity but would still require a substantial role in management.

When is it most appropriate?

Unlike public share offerings, trade sales are typically carried out with minimal legal restructuring, require less planning and are thus cheaper and faster to execute. This does not mean that they are not complex in their own right - because the (large) companies that are sold through a trade sale are often not fit for an IPO. In terms of prerequisites, trade sales also have the advantage of being feasible in the absence of a well-developed and sophisticated market environment.

A key specific benefit of a trade sale is the experience and know-how that a strategic or financial investor might bring. For this reason it is often used for the sale of small- and medium-sized companies and in companies that might benefit from the introduction of strong management and infusion of technology. Another potential benefit is that it can provide an avenue for promoting foreign direct investment, if this is a broader governmental objective.

Figure 3.2. Private sale process and timeline: Case example from Sweden

The private sales process in Sweden typically takes four months to execute and involves preparation for the sale; a first round of negotiations; a second round of negotiations with buyers and final negotiations where the bidder is selected and the sale is concluded.

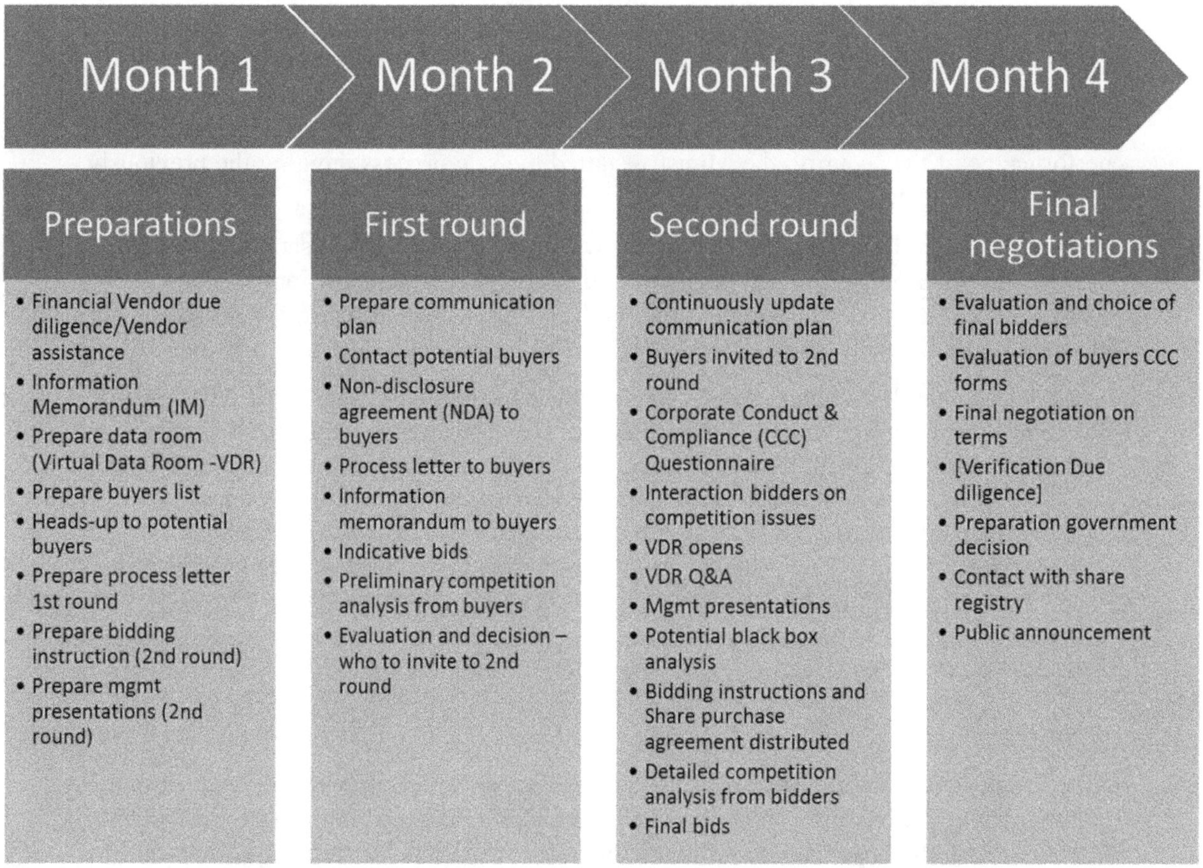

Source: Submission from Swedish authorities.

It should also be noted that the state might pursue a dual track sale - in other words starting the process of privatisation with either a trade sale or IPO in mind. It can then decide on which process will be suitable and render the best price. A trade sale also costs less than an IPO and can thus be more cost-effective depending on the size and value of the company.

Disadvantages?

The sale of a stake to a strategic investor may not bring in the strict governance regime that a listed company needs to comply with, although it has to be noted that many such investors do impose such standards and discipline either because they are listed themselves in their home market or in some cases by virtue of their global/international profile.

In terms of process integrity the main drawback is that trade sales do not provide the same degree of transparency as public offerings and therefore they may potentially be prone to corruption, in particular when they are conducted through non-competitive processes. In this context a fully transparent process and the establishment of clear and detailed procedures for conducting negotiations and selecting buyers can go a long way in alleviating such concerns and help protect the integrity of the process.

The two main factors that may militate against trade sales of an entire enterprise are: (1) competition concerns related to the combined market share of the acquirer; and (2) the case where the SOE to be privatised is very large relative to the size of domestic (or, if the SOE operates internationally, relevant) markets and existing competitors.

How does it work?

There are two main types of trade sales used in privatisations: auctions (competitive bidding) and negotiated sales. Auctions have been more common and may be considered more transparent than negotiated sales. It is up to the government, the company and their advisors to choose the method most suited to the case at hand. Irrespective of the method chosen, it is vital for the process to be conducted in an organised and transparent manner, balancing revenue maximisation with other policy objectives.

Negotiated sales

Under this approach, the government has the flexibility to negotiate with buyers individually and to present a different set of conditions to each. This option might be well-suited where there are relatively small equity markets, and the number of potential buyers for an asset is limited thus rendering a competitive sale process uneconomic. The main drawback however is the possible lack of transparency. For this reason, the selection process must be transparent and clear rules need to be established to mitigate against the potential risk and perception of abuse.

Auctions (competitive bidding process)

The other approach to trade sales is through a competitive bidding process. This approach can take two forms. First, it can take the form of a simple price-based competitive bidding process where price is the sole criteria for the sale. The second approach involves a competition for a business plan design and an evaluation of the bid based on a combination of factors and not just price. Factors that may influence the choice of one method versus another include: the size of the asset; the nature of the product market and whether there is adequate competition; and the extent to which there may be continued need for public policy objectives such as universal service obligations.

Figure 3.3. Planning the IPO process

A carefully planned and executed flotation process is critical to the success to the initial public offering and successive offerings

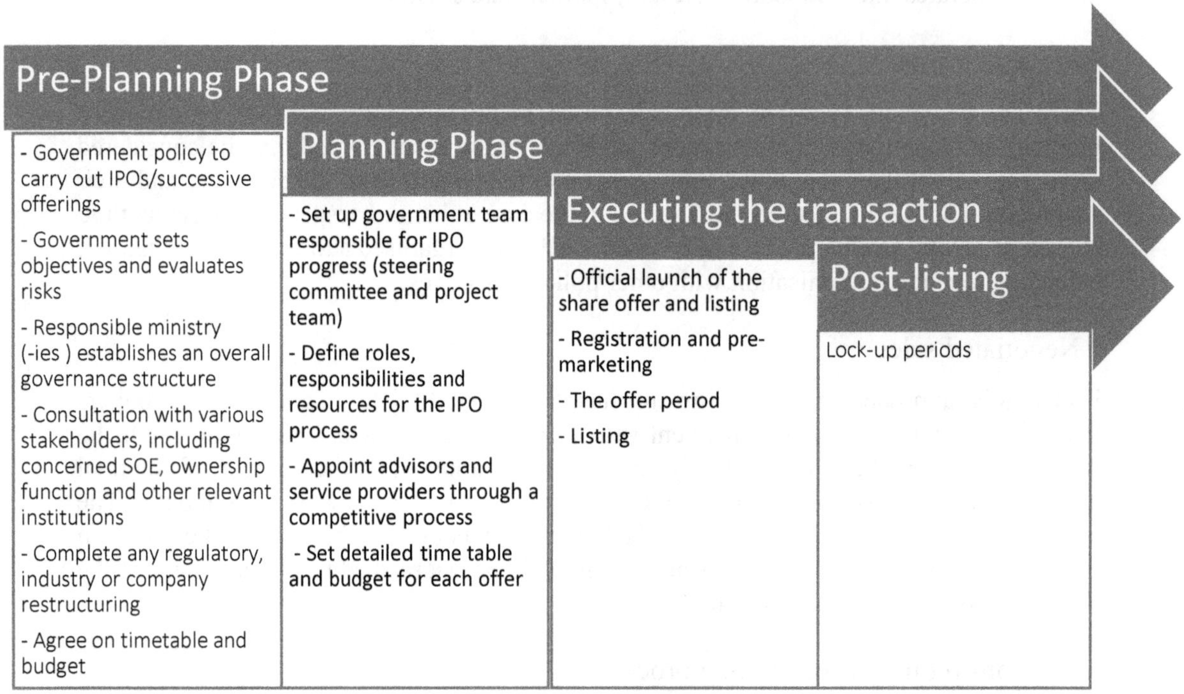

Source: Adapted from OECD (2016).

Box 3.8. Special section on public share offerings

Governments usually do not sell an entire SOE or even a controlling stake in an SOE in the initial offering. The main dividing line among government owners relates to whether the intent behind an IPO is an eventual full privatisation, a continued state majority ownership, or a significant minority ownership. Hybrid approaches are of course possible: some governments, at the time of IPO, defer decisions regarding possible secondary and tertiary offerings to a later date. The division can be described thus as follows:

- **Continued government control of the listed entity is foreseen.** In this case the main motives behind listing can be purely fiscal, or may reflect a strategy of relying on market mechanisms to lift the SOEs' corporate performance.
- **IPO is seen as the first tranche of a full privatisation**. Large SOEs are usually privatised through listing rather than trade-sales. The pace of the privatisation process (i.e. of subsequent share offerings) may depend on a number of factors:
    - **Going slow.** Where the SOE to be privatised is large relative to domestic capital markets there is a clear case for going slow in order to obtain the best price. Also, a gradual process allows time to upgrade corporate governance and regulatory frameworks, thus further boosting the valuation of the company. OECD (2009) showed that the largest privatisation proceeds from SOEs in the utilities sectors normally derive from the tertiary share offering.
    - **Going fast.** If capital markets are liquid and have a high absorption capacity, and if the privatised company is perceived as well managed, then there is little

incentive for governments to drag out the privatisation process. Some delays may, however, be necessary for practical reasons, such as settling legacy contractual and staff issues.

When going to the stock market the government owner will be confronted with a series of decisions as to how to price and market its company's shares, how to transfer control and how to allocate shares. Unlike private sector issuers, governments may pursue listing with different objectives than private issuers. This may be influenced by both economic and political factors, and governments may approach listing by placing various weights on these two competing goals. The relative importance of each goal is determined by the country's unique motivation to list (i.e. historical, cultural, fiscal, etc.), which may have an impact on the pace, scope and structure of the listing process.

According to OECD (2016), over 90% of share-issue privatisations are oversubscribed. This is attributed to the fact that governments' share allocations almost always guarantee significant portions of the offers to domestic and retail investors, as opposed to foreign and institutional investors. By discounting stock, governments also indicate that they are willing to accept lower proceeds resulting from privatisation. On the one hand, this can result in the IPO being criticised by opponents of privatisation, since in some cases discounted stock can give the impression that SOEs are offered for less than market value. On the other hand, it may provide political support for the process, and attract a larger share of domestic ownership, which may also help achieve other goals such as developing local stock markets. Discounting shares for employees may also build further support for privatisation with labour unions or employees.

On the flip side, government officials may pursue higher prices as a strategy to maximise proceeds from privatisation to meet specific fiscal objectives. Countries with less developed capital markets are more likely to discount shares in IPOs to promote broader share ownership

Generally, the benefits of listing can only be reaped in an environment where the stock market and legal system are sufficiently functional to establish effective corporate governance that protects the interests of all shareholders, especially minority shareholders (Wang et al., 2004). In other words, the intensity of capital market pressure will also depend on the extent to which individual shareholder rights are protected and enforced; and the extent to which the disciplining effect of non-state shareholders may be felt more strongly. The performance benefits yielded by going to the market should also be weighed with the level of market competition and deregulation.

Source: OECD (2016).

Management and employee buy-out

What is it?

Management and employee buy-outs (MEBOs) typically refer to privatisation through the sale of the enterprise to a new legal entity in which a significant, or majority, stake is owned by the employees and managers. The buyers may be only employees, or only managers, or a mix of the two. The transfer could involve all or part of the assets or shares in the company and the method by which the sale is financed may or may not involve a commitment of funds by the employees and managers.

When is it most appropriate?

It has been widely argued that the introduction of a significant amount of insider equity ownership can have a positive effect on corporate governance and efficiency in that it leads to closer monitoring of performance and helps align the employee and management incentives with those of the owners (converts agents into principals). Governments might encourage MEBOs as a means of improving corporate efficiency and gaining employee support for privatisation. MEBOs also tend to be suited to smaller companies.

Disadvantages?

This approach to sale can also have corporate governance weaknesses in that insiders may seek to pursue objectives such as job security and job-based utility and forgo the increase in the value of the company. This could be particularly the case where the acquisition of the stake has not involved a financial commitment by this group of buyers (i.e. the stake has been a giveaway) and where effective external monitoring by outsiders and hard budget constraints (e.g. through the lending financial institutions and the need to meet debt service payments) is absent. It also can restrict access to capital: if the business is acquired by its management team without the support of a financial investor, it may not be easy to raise equity if it's needed. Furthermore, where employees are a heterogeneous group in terms of their skills, interests and objectives, effective decision-making can be hampered as a result of the need to reconcile conflicting objectives.

How does it work?

The transfer of part or all of the assets can take place through a purchase of the company by employees, management or both. In some cases the shares can either be given away or purchased by the employees/management. Financial institutions can also be involved as a source of credit or as buyers.

MEBOs are most often considered as part of a broader privatisation process whereby part of the stake in the company is sold to management and/or employees, with the remainder of the sale taking place through a negotiated sale, or as part of a competitive process.

Mixed sale

What is it?

Mixed sales typically combine trade sales with a public share offering and/or the sale of stakes to employees. In a mixed sale, privatisation usually begins with the transfer of some degree of control (66% of voting rights, i.e. a super majority; 51% absolute majority; or some relative majority, e.g. 33.5%) to a strategic buyer. It is then followed by the public offering of shares on the stock market. A third possible component is the placement of some portion of shares with the company employees, as a means of ensuring worker participation.

When is it appropriate?

Through this approach governments are able to achieve multiple objectives. For example, with a trade sale the company may undergo management changes and restructuring required before being publicly traded. After the new ownership structure has improved efficiency and created value in the company, further privatisation can possibly secure higher share prices in subsequent tranches. Furthermore, by having the trade sale precede the public offering, the government is likely to obtain a better price for the stakes sold than if it were to do it once the shares have been trading in the stock market, depending on how share price is determined.

Disadvantages?

A mixed process takes longer, will require additional advisory services and can be costly to execute. Furthermore, the success of a multiple-staged process, which culminates with a public listing, will require that the first stage of privatisation goes smoothly.

How does it work?

The order by which the different sale methods are combined varies. It is most common that the sale to a strategic investor precedes the public offering of shares. The success of this strategy is critically dependent on the government's ability to ensure that good corporate governance practices are in place to protect minority shareholders. In the absence of such practices, shareholders might be abused by the controllers and as a result public offerings will lose credibility with damaging effects on capital market development.

Convertible bond

What is it?

A convertible bond gives the bond holder the option to exchange the bond for a predetermined number of shares in the issuing company. The issue of convertible bonds is a means to collect capital at a lower cost than the issue of ordinary bonds[3]. The issue price and nominal yield are set in advance which presupposes an implicit share value.

When is it appropriate?

This option is suitable to dispose of minority blocks and thus offers the possibility to gradually privatise. It can lend credibility to the government's willingness to dispose of its share in the company and thus generate positive expectations on the company's share value. Governments might resort to the issuance of convertible bonds also in times of stock market weakness (Ruozi, 1999).

In some jurisdictions it can support corporate governance reform and better financial discipline given the bond payment obligations that ensue before conversion to common stock. According to Ma (2004), Chinese companies have reportedly found convertible bonds easier to launch than share-purchase rights or additional share offerings, reflecting the character of the Chinese stock market and legal and regulatory environment. For example, convertible bond floor price attracts investor participation, which results in less underwriting risk as compared to common stock offerings. In earlier privatisation experiences of some European economies, convertible bonds were also used as an antecedent to privatisation via IPO.

Demerits?

This is a complex instrument and is not commonly used as a privatisation method. From the perspective of the seller, a demerit is that the investor decides when to exercise the conversion option (that is, when the option becomes exercisable). If the stock poorly performs, there is no conversion and an investor is stuck with the bond's sub-par return (below what a non-convertible corporate bond would get); and ultimately the government does not achieve its objective to shed ownership gradually.

How does it work?

When issued it is just like a regular corporate bond, but with a lower interest rate. It postpones transfer of ownership for a period of time determined by the investor exercising the conversion option.

Ensuring effective communication, transparency and integrity of the process

Privatisation can be a contentious process in that it: brings about changes that erode the influence of bureaucrats and SOE managers; involves restructuring and the potential for loss of jobs; and has an impact on consumers for whom price and access to goods and services are likely to be altered. Therefore, it can face opposition from various stakeholders. Furthermore, privatisations give rise to risks of potential abuse by the participants in the process. This can severely undermine government credibility and set back reform efforts. For this reason, the communication and transparency around the transaction or broader privatisation programme should serve to enhance its integrity and gain credibility with potential investors and ensure public support. The government must also undertake key measures to ensure the integrity of individual transactions (covered in more detail in the special section below. See also Annex A).

One communication strategy that governments use is to ensure continuous and real-time information access on the privatisation process through online platforms. This is in particular practiced in jurisdictions where there is a complex privatisation programme involving a large number of transactions. For example, in Kazakhstan the Committee on State Property and Privatisation under the Ministry of Finance has created a special web-site publishing the main information on the performance, audit reports and number of employees of entities being privatised. Notification on bids are also posted for access by the general public.[4]

With regard to potential abuse of the transaction, special care should be taken to avoid collusion on the selling price between the buyer and the government official in charge of the privatisation. To mitigate these risks some jurisdictions have set up specialised privatisation commissions where the members are independent and can have no link with the transaction (see Box 3.9).

Box 3.9. Oversight of privatisation transactions: Case example from France

In France a designated Shareholdings and Transfers Commission, made of up independent experts, is a body responsible for ensuring the integrity of privatisation transactions. Its role is to protect public assets, make the selection of buyers transparent, ensure that company valuation and price setting are done in a transparent manner (in some cases it also sets the price), give opinions on sales and offer ex-post evaluations of privatisations.

The Commission is made up of seven members. Members are appointed for a non-renewable six-year term of office by Prime Ministerial decree and are chosen "for their economic, financial and legal skills and experience".

Commission members must abide by certain rules to ensure their independence:

- They are bound by professional secrecy.
- Their duties "are incompatible with any tenure as member of a board of directors or supervisory board of a joint-stock corporation or any paid activity for such a company liable to make them dependent on any buyers".
- For a period of five years following the end of their duties, they cannot "become a member of a board of directors or supervisory board of a company, or any of its subsidiaries, that has bid for shareholdings previously held by the government and cannot carry out a paid activity for such companies".

The Commission, acting on behalf of the majority of its members (the chairman casts the deciding vote in the event of a tie), will remove any member who does not comply with the first two requirements above. Immediately upon taking office and for the term's duration, all members must inform the chairman of their professional activities, positions held as corporate officers and any groups that they may represent. The very restrictive incompatibility rules are such that appointments generally go to individuals who are no longer directly involved in business activities.

The compensation and fees paid to Commission members are made public. A General Secretariat organises the work and prepares the Commission's examination of the dossiers. The General Secretary is appointed by decision of the Minister for the Economy based on a proposal from the Commission chairman.

Source: Commission des Participations et des Transferts (2016).

Box 3.10. Special section on anti-corruption and integrity in the privatisation process

This special section addresses the particular risks of corruption and rule breaking in each stage of the privatisation process and identifies red flags that policy makers should consider in each step of the privatisation process. A step-by-step guide is provided in Annex A.

SOEs are considered at risk of corruption for their common operation in high-risk sectors (e.g. extractive and network industries), engagement in high-value public procurements and inherent ties to public and political officials through their complex ownership structures. In particular, fraudulent activity and receiving bribes are considered most likely to occur and most impactful on SOEs (OECD, 2018, 2014; TI, 2017). Some consider privatisation as a policy lever for reducing the heightened corruption risks of the SOE sector. However, research shows that the effect of privatisation on corruption is inconclusive[5]. This is partly owing to the fact that the effect of privatisation on corruption will depend on the nature of the corruption risks facing SOEs, which are in turn partly dependent on the sector of operation and the social, economic and political context of the country. SOEs can be perpetrators of corrupt acts or conduits of abuse that can be facilitated or exacerbated by state ownership. Privatisation may reduce opportunities for rent seeking but does not deal with actors inclined to rent-seek within the political, public or private sectors.

Privatisation itself can be instrumentalised for personal or political gain: its vulnerability partly stemming from the large number of assets being transferred into private hands and through the spill over of the very behaviour that threatens the SOE sector. There are two main entry points of corruption in privatisation (Emmanuel, A. and S. Straub, 2011). First, corruption or undue influence can lead to a misinformed decision to privatise or the wrong candidate being selected for privatisation (for instance, the selloff of highly profitable monopolies), explored less in existing literature. Second, the right candidate may be chosen for privatisation but corruption threatens success and distorts the efficiency, effectiveness and economy of the process for the benefit of a few.

Managing corruption risks and red flags in the privatisation process

Guiding Principles. The decision to privatise is taken in a context of evolving governmental priorities, political cycles and changing paradigms about the value of public ownership. Measures must be taken to ensure that corruption – the abuse of power for personal or political gain – is not also a deciding factor. The risk of undue influence may be heightened where decisions need to be taken regarding sectors that are highly regulated, or conversely where regulatory capacity is lagging, with a large number of public policy objectives or where there are natural market monopolies and/or high-value public procurements. Adoption of the guiding principles outlined in Chapter 2 can help to reduce the risk of rent-seeking behaviour and undue influence in key decisions about privatisation.

Measures before divesting. The steps taken prior to divestment by both the company and public authorities are critical for ensuring success of the process. A transaction can fail well before it is executed. It is in this phase that upstream decisions are taken about the method of sale, industry is accorded adequate checks and balances and due diligence is undertaken on the candidate company. It is thus in this stage that corrupt actors may seek to manipulate the establishment of needed checks and balances that in order to increase rents and mask the eventual diversion of resources for personal or political gain. For instance, the selection of the method of sale could be influenced by their intrinsic degrees of transparency. IPOs are arguably the most transparent while direct sales are the least transparent. The seller needs to be mindful of the differences and adopt an appropriate risk mitigation strategy. If the seller reverts to trade sale or employee buyout, which may have less process integrity, additional safeguards may be required. Moreover, the selloff of a monopoly without structural separation can facilitate the abuse of a market dominant position and monopolistic rents.

Organising the process of privatisation. The actual process of privatisation should be steered by a centralised organ and may involve advice from an external party. Decisions must be taken about company valuation and potential buyers, and bids are handled. Adherence to good practices in the execution of privatisation, covered earlier, mitigates the risk of manipulating criteria for selloff, and distorting a fair bidding and awarding process. Corruption and bribery can threaten a fair acquisition price. One study found that privatisation by states that appear more corrupt will have a higher acquisition price (Bjorvatn, K. and T. Søreide, 2005). Collusion and bid-rigging will thwart fair competition. Finally, risks may arise through conflicts of interest or undue influence by external advisors (covered in Chapter 4).

Taking steps post-privatisation. Accountability is needed following the transaction to handle residual guarantees or liabilities and proceeds. Evaluation will assess compliance with the terms of privatisation that may include assessment of performance in the delivery of public services. Ex-post audit will assess propriety and value for money. Adherence to good practices in this phase, as outlined in Chapter 5, is doubly important for (i) its potential to detect irregularities in the privatisation process and (ii) providing ongoing assurance for upholding contractual terms and appropriate handling of profits from the divestment. Efforts may be made to influence any of these steps in order to mask a corruption scheme.

Source: Secretariat.

Notes

[1] It should be noted that listing requirements vary across jurisdictions and in some cases can be used as a reason to "shop around" for the lightest criteria.

[2] Discounting stock price is a technique that may be used to provide political support for the process, and attract a larger share of domestic ownership, which may also benefit other goals such as developing local stock markets - this is particularly the case for countries with less developed capital markets. Discounting shares for employees may also build further support for privatisation with labour unions or employees. On the other hand, research by Pargendler et al. (2013) does not agree with the hypothesis that SOE share prices are "discounted" on the basis that private investors may be willing to accept risks of government involvement, and that the very nature of state participation can guarantee a steady supply of rents from its (sometimes) monopolistic exploitation of natural resources and public concessions. This is particularly the case in the oil sector.

[3] However, convertibles are often more expensive than ordinary bonds when you take into account the cost of the equity option.

[4] http://privatization.gosreestr.kz/en.

[5] Existing literature has focused largely on the residual impact of privatisation on the economy, including on corruption. Studies are conflictual, with some finding it can reduce corruption and others that it can increase corruption, some finding no effect and others that it depends on timing and context (for instance, see Cuadrado-Ballesteros, B. and N. Peña Miguel (2018), Koyuncu, C., H. Ozturkler and R. Yilmaz (2010), Ramlogan-Dobson, C. and A Rodriguez (2008)).

References

Auriol, E. and S. Straub (2011), "Privatization of rent-generating industries and corruption, International Handbook on the Economics of Corruption", Volume Two, https://www.researchgate.net/profile/Emmanuelle_Auriol/publication/286050256_Privatization_of_rent-generating_industries_and_corruption/links/586b627708aebf17d3a588a7/Privatization-of-rent-generating-industries-and-corruption.pdf?origin=publication_detail.

Bjorvatn, K. and T. Søreide (2005), Corruption and privatization, European Journal of Political Economy, https://doi.org/10.1016/j.ejpoleco.2005.02.001.

Commission des Participations et des Transfers (2016), "The Holdings and Transfers Commission and Privatisations in France", March 2016.

Cuadrado-Ballesteros, B. and N. Peña Miguel (2018), "Is privatization related to corruption? An empirical analysis of European countries", *Public Management Review*, Doi:10.1080/14719037.2018.1444192

European Commission (2012), "Guidance Paper on state aid-compliant financing, restructuring and privatisation of State-owned enterprises", *Commission Staff Working Document*, http://ec.europa.eu/competition/state_aid/studies_reports/swd_guidance_paper_en.pdf.

International Organisation of Supreme Audit Institutions (1998), "Guidelines on Best Practice for the Audit of Privatisations – ISSAI 5210", International Standards of Supreme Audit Institutions, www.issai.org/en_us/site-issai/issai-framework/4-auditing-guidelines.htm.

Jones, S., Megginson, W., Nash, R. C. and Netter, J. M. (1999), "Share issue privatizations as financial means to political and economic ends", *Journal of Financial Economic*, 53, 217-253.

Koyuncu, C., H. Ozturkler and R. Yilmaz (2010), "Privatization and corruption in transition economies: A panel study", *Journal of Economic Policy Reform*, https://www.researchgate.net/publication/227347872

Ma W. (2004), "Convertible Bonds: A New Approach to China's Stock Markets", *UC Davis Business Law Journal*, Volume 5, Issue 1.

OECD (2018a), Privatisation and the Broadening of Ownership of SOEs: Stocktaking of National Practices, https://www.oecd.org/daf/ca/Privatisation-and-the-Broadening-of-Ownership-of-SOEs-Stocktaking-of-National-Practices.pdf.

OECD (2018b), State-Owned Enterprises and Corruption: What Are the Risks and What Can Be Done?, https://doi.org/10.1787/9789264303058-en.

OECD (2016), Broadening the Ownership of State-Owned Enterprises: A Comparison of Governance Practices, OECD Publishing, Paris. http://dx.doi.org/10.1787/9789264244603-en.

OECD (2015), *OECD Guidelines on Corporate Governance of State-Owned Enterprises*, 2015 Edition, http://dx.doi.org/10.1787/9789264244160-en.

OECD (2014), *OECD Foreign Bribery Report: An Analysis of the Crime of Bribery of Foreign Public Officials*, www.oecd.org/corruption/oecd-foreign-briberyreport-9789264226616-en.htm.

OECD (2012), *Competitive Neutrality: Maintaining a Level Playing Field between Public and Private Business*, OECD Publishing, Paris. http://dx.doi.org/10.1787/9789264178953-en

OECD (2010), Privatisation in the 21st Century: *Summary of Recent Experiences*, https://www.oecd.org/daf/ca/corporategovernanceofstate-ownedenterprises/43449100.pdf.

OECD (2009), Privatisation in the 21st Century*: Recent Experiences of OECD Countries: Report on Good Practices*, January 2009, https://www.oecd.org/daf/ca/corporategovernanceofstate-ownedenterprises/48476423.pdf.

OECD (2003), *Privatising State-Owned Enterprises: An Overview of Policies and Practices in OECD Countries*, OECD Publishing, Paris, https://doi.org/10.1787/9789264104099-en.

Pargendler, M., Musacchio, A. M. and Lazzarini, S. G. (2013), "In Strange Company: The Puzzle of Private Investment in State-Controlled Firms", *Harvard Business School Working Paper*, No. 13–071, February 2013.

Ramlogan-Dobson, C. and A Rodriguez (2008), "Corruption, privatisation and the distribution of income in Latin America," Nottingham Trent University, Discussion Paper in Economics, https://www.ntu.ac.uk/__data/assets/pdf_file/0016/310255/Corruption-privatisation-and-the-distribution-of-income.pdf

Ruozi R. and Anderloni L. (eds.) (1999), "Banking Privatisation in Europe - The Process and the Consequences on Strategies and Organisational Structures", Springer-Verlag, Berlin Heidelberg.

Transparency International (TI) (2017), "10 Anti-Corruption Principles for State-Owned Enterprises", Berlin, https://www.transparency.org/whatwedo/publication/10_anti_corruption_principles_for_state_owned_enterprises

Chapter 4. Organising the process of privatisation

The actual process of privatising state-owned enterprises (or parts of them) involves both decision-making within the state and practical measures undertaken by state-owned enterprises themselves, in consultation with external advisors. This chapter covers the following aspects: effectively steering the process to see through the transaction; best practices for drawing upon external advice; determining company valuation and establishing sound pricing methods; determining potential buyers and handling bids; and, active and on-going communication with stakeholders and the public.

The actual process of privatising state-owned enterprises (SOEs) (or parts of them) involves both decision-making within the state and practical measures undertaken by SOEs themselves, in consultation with external advisors. This chapter will cover the following aspects: effectively steering the process to see through the transaction; best practices for drawing upon external advice; determining company valuation and establishing sound pricing methods; determining potential buyers and handling bids; and, active and on-going communication with stakeholders and the public.

Effectively steering the process to see through the transaction

The state-ownership entity or other assigned entity to oversee the transaction should establish an organ (typically a steering group and a project group) to oversee the privatisation transaction, organisation and planning. This body will be responsible for the actual implementation of the transaction and will be the main body responsible for the selection of transaction advisors, communication strategy, consultation process (if required), and making decisions as to the staging and sequencing of the privatisation process. It will interact with the external advisors as well as directly with the SOE. Finally, the role of the steering group will be to interact with ministers to facilitate quick decision-making (See also Chapter 2).

The roles and responsibilities of various stakeholders involved in the privatisation process should be clearly defined at all stages of the process, and especially during the process to see through the transaction. These stakeholders may include the ownership entity, in a steering role, the company (board and management) if the transaction is of a wholly-owned entity, external advisors hired by the ownership entity, and if relevant, those hired by the SOE.

Importantly, for individual transactions involving wholly-owned SOEs the steering group should also involve the external advisors and key members of the board and management in the steering group (see also Box 2.6 with case example from Norway), as the company board and management of wholly-owned SOEs will play a key role in ensuring the company's "readiness" for privatisation. This includes getting the company's affairs "in order". Key decisions will need to be made in terms of the company's strategy, capital structure; corporate governance frameworks, etc. (see also Chapter 3 for more in-depth coverage of "readiness").

Regular meetings of the steering group should take place and depending on the topic at hand will involve the input of different stakeholders more. For example, where the discussion may be focused on the current dividend policy, the ownership may take a more active role in the steering group; whereas if the discussion is focused on restructuring the company, for example what assets will be included in the sale, then the management will work closely with the advisors to "work through" those issues and develop and equity story and clear strategy to go to the market (see Box 4.1 for case example from Norway).

Care should be taken from the outset that the various roles and competencies of each stakeholder involved in the transaction are carefully considered. Where other parts of government are involved, or if Parliamentary consultation is required, potential for micro-management of an individual transaction should be avoided, which can potentially undermine the sale parameters or divulge information that would otherwise need to be kept confidential.

Box 4.1. Sales of Entra: Case example from Norway

In 2014, the Norwegian authorities undertook a privatisation (IPO) of the real estate company Entra ASA. Leading up to stock listing of the company, the government spent three to four years discussing the company's portfolio before pursuing a dual-track offering (M&A and IPO). The discussions took place within the Government and between the ownership entity and the company. The government had as an objective to get the maximum value for the company and it was important to develop a clear equity story and strategy before going to the market. As such it was important to decide what part of the portfolio of real estate assets would be in included in the sale. This process was lengthy and involved many discussions to work through a strategy.

Ultimately, in 2014 the reals estate company was listed on the stock exchange through an IPO, including 50.4% of the company's shares. This transaction brought the state around USD 450 million in revenue. In September 2016, the Norwegian state, represented by the Ministry of Trade, Industry and Fisheries completed a secondary placement of 30 million shares in Entra ASA, representing 16.3% of the share capital and voting rights in the company. Following completion of the placement, the government will own 33.4% of the share capital and voting rights in the company. Proceeds from the share placement amounted to around USD 319 million.

Source: Submission by the Norwegian authorities.

Best practices for drawing upon external advice

Privatisation is a resource intensive activity, often demanding skills and expertise that require outside expertise. As experience from the OECD countries shows, most privatisation transactions have included some degree of involvement of external advisors (Figure 4.1). Typically, the hiring of advisors is one of the tasks carried out during the very early stages of the programme. Depending on the size of the SOE, and the complexity of the transaction (e.g. IPO), the SOE may hire its own advisors, including financial advisors and management consultants. The government owner, too, will have its own advisors to provide legal counsel, accounting and financial advice, strategic and transactional advice provided by investment banks, and advertising and PR firms for what concerns communication, market research and the public relations campaign. In this regard, the government and the SOE need to ensure that they are not hiring the same advisory firms to avoid conflicts of interest. This is especially important if the company already has outside shareholders, and the transaction represents a secondary or tertiary offering, for example.

Developing the expertise in selecting and monitoring the performance of advisors has proven to be an important consideration in preparing for privatisation. Given that privatisation often entails a large degree of interface with advisors, it is important to ensure that in-house expertise in the ownership/privatisation unit/agency is cultivated. This also underscores the benefit of a centralised approach to managing privatisation in that this approach tends to lower costs and improves the chances of developing such capability.

The planning and implementation of privatisation involve a significant amount of interaction, which requires a great deal of planning and effective coordination of a large number of critical and interdependent policy and transactional tasks in order for transactions to be carried out under favourable market conditions and at the optimal time.

Three distinct phases can be distinguished: (i) the pre-sale phase; (ii) the sale preparation phase; and (iii) the sale process phases. Each phase necessitates a different level of advisory services, and the mode of sale will also determine exactly which advisory services will be necessary.

Pre-sale phase

One of the first steps in privatisation of a SOE is corporatisation whereby the SOE is typically converted to a joint stock company whose shares are held by the government. Legal and financial advisors are hired to advise on corporatisation and on preparation of enabling legislation where this is required.

During the early stages of the sale where the asset is valued and method of sale is being discussed, a number of external advisors are hired (e.g. financial advisors, accounting firms, lawyers, communication firms, etc.). They advise on a wide range of issues. For example, they might advise on how best to position the asset; the timing of the privatisation; valuation of the firm using different valuation methodologies; feasibility of the sale and the most appropriate method of the sale and the possible markets; research on possible buyers. The advisors will also determine the "readiness" of the company to be privatised.

Often based on this type of advice, and depending on their approach to selling, the government makes a decision in principle regarding the key parameters of the transaction and whether or not the process moves on to the implementation aspects of the sale. However caution should be exercised during this stage, as advisors should fully understand the objectives of the government at the time of privatisation. These objectives will vary according to the company, market conditions and the method of sale (see also Chapter 2 on rationales for privatisation). Caution should also be exercised to ensure that advisory services are not driven by perverse incentives.

Sale preparation phase

During the sale preparation phase financial advisors are hired to review the SOE's business and finances, its accounting practices and to advise on matters such as preparation of the company books (which should have already been subject to audit), valuation and financial restructuring. While most transactions require the services of financial advisors, the range and the sophistication of advisory services required is determined by the size and complexity of the transaction. The method of sale matters as a trade sale requires less preparation and restructuring than a public share offering. The sale of larger assets and especially those operating in non-competitive sectors of the economy generally involves company-specific restructuring, and in the case of the latter, sector restructuring as well. In this context, management consultants and industry experts are hired to advise on restructuring.

Sale process

During the sale process the financial advisors such as investment banks are hired as part of the book building process, and to solicit interest from potential buyers, preparing the transaction documents and helping market the company to the potential investors. A number of countries also rely on more specialised outside advice, such as vendor due diligence and in some cases even public relations services. In preparing the prospectus the government needs to work closely with its legal, financial and sale advisors, as well as with the company and its financial and legal advisors. Most governments hire separate advisors for advisory and sale mandates to ensure there is no conflict of interest between the two (although for secondary offerings this is less of a problem).

Figure 4.1. Role of external advisors for government and SOE

Aspects of the privatisation process are informed by or assigned to external advisors. Often the SOE and the ownership entity will be advised separately depending on the method of sale.

Source: Adapted from OECD (2003).

Selection of advisors and avoiding conflicts of interest

Transparency around the selection of advisors

Transparency of the process helps ensure that decisions are not arbitrary and have been based according to certain rules and criteria, and are applied in a fair and open manner. For this reason, a precise and clear set of rules and procedures are defined and followed. Establishment of clear rules and processes for auctions, specific criteria for the evaluation process in the context of competitive bidding, use of open procedures in the selection of private sector advisors, and rigorous publicity requirements contribute to the acceptability of the process by making sure that the choices have not been driven by vested interests and that they have been arrived at in the context of a level playing field.

In order to ensure best value and to protect the transparency of the privatisation process, governments should hire advisors through a competitive bidding process. Given the importance of technical/specialised skills, the competitive processes should give sufficient weight to the quality, competence, and experience of advisors as the key criteria in the selection. In this regard, it would be useful to develop a list of qualified bidders instead of focusing exclusively on cost. Moreover, this should be worked into the public procurement process to ensure that the government can hire the best advisors and not those which pitch the lowest price and possibly with conflicted interests.

There are exceptions from procurement law when procuring investment banks. For example, in Sweden the Swedish Procurement Act provides for exceptions, *inter alia* when procuring financial advisors in connection with share divestments, although the EU principles of equal treatment and non-discrimination still apply. The ownership entity has a public list of all interested banks from which a few advisors are selected through objective criteria and invited to compete for the assignment. Final evaluation is performed on price and quality. For other types of services EU procurement law applies and specific framework agreements apply (for legal, communication, strategy consultants etc.).[1]

Conflicts of interest

Conflict of interest provisions for government officials, SOE insiders, and private agents, are measures that can help ensure that the rules are applied uniformly and thus enhance transparency. This can assure investors and the public that the decisions are based on the established criteria, and through maximum disclosure the government can contribute to the process integrity and stem public criticism of the process. Often the potential for conflicts of interest is very real and therefore measures aimed at mitigating against them are needed to ensure the integrity of the process. In this respect, the rules should focus on intra-corporate relationships, especially regarding SOEs, activities of government officials and the behaviour of sub-contractors.

Advisors will also be subject to a confidentiality/non-disclosure agreement to ensure that their involvement in the privatisation transaction does not compromise the sale nor the bargaining position of the seller (Box 4.2).

Box 4.2. Hiring external advisors: Case example from Italy

In preparing and executing privatization deals, the Italian Ministry of Economy and Finance is authorised by the law to select a group of advisors with proven national or international experience in kind of activities like: economic research, consultancy, evaluation, operational assistance and management of placement transactions. Furthermore, such process must always take into account the restrictions coming from conflicts of interest or incompatibility for previous or current mandates.

For instance, in operations carried out through global offers, a primary role is played by the experience of consultants who are requested to support the seller in the placement procedure on international financial markets.

In this context, the first phase is focused on the search of financial and/or legal advisors who will take part in all the preliminary and preparatory steps to carry out the operation. The selection is made on the basis of the criteria established to determine the most favourable tender taking into consideration, in addition to the price offered, the wide credentials of entity. Therefore, the experience gained by the financial institution/law firm, the quality and experience of the working group and the fees required are all carefully measured, with different degrees related to the complexity and the size of the privatization.

The selection for choosing the advisors starts with the letter containing an official invitation to present the formal offers. Usually, such letter is addressed to up to 10-15 entities, which are identified starting from their track records proven by international league tables. For answers arrived before the deadline (generally ten working days after the invitation letter), a first screening is made with respect to the absence of conflicts of interest, even only potential.

In the offer submitted to the Ministry of Economy and Finance, the bidders have to:

- declare the absence of any conflict of interest
- list actual consultancy appointments with subsidiaries of the Ministry of Economy and Finance, which may present incompatibility profiles with the perspective mandate
- undersign a commitment to accept the main contractual clauses, including the confidentiality agreement.

The offers are then carefully evaluated and the overall assessment is expressed with ranking from 1 to 10, which will result from the sum of the following specific features, variously weighted:

- experience gained by the financial institution/law firm for each operation, with special focus on: a) the most recent transactions (from 3 up to 5 years); b) deals involving companies operating in the same sector of activity in which the company operates; c) general IPO/privatization
- quality and expertise of the team, (i.e. for each team member an assessment of 1 to 10 is assigned, with regard mainly to the role held, the seniority and the experience)
- competitiveness of the tender, where the evaluation derives from a comparison of the fees requested by all the bidders involved.

However, the remuneration of the advisors will depend on the general role played through different phases of the deal and, in the past, the compensation structure has been linked to the size of transaction or to the specific activity of the advisory. At the end, the Ministry of Economy and Finance communicates to the market the winner of the selection by a press release. Costs of the advisor services are usually paid by the proceeds coming from the divestment.

Source: Submission from Italian authorities

Accountability

Accountability of privatisation institutions helps enhance the integrity of the privatisation process. The mechanism for ensuring accountability is largely shaped by the existing arrangements and institutions that are in place in each country, and whether they are deemed to be adequate for addressing privatisation transactions, and the need to balance accountability requirements (to the executive branch and/or legislature) against the potential for rendering the process excessively vulnerable to short-term political consideration. In most countries, and according to best practices, the national audit institution will perform an ex-post audit to privatisation transactions.

Often the selling price is one of the main sources of criticism. The approach to ensuring proper pricing has varied among different OECD countries, but some countries have used "reservation prices" as a bottom limit to the amount of a sale. As for perverse incentives for the transaction not to be overpriced, the government should be aware of the incentive structure of advisors and market conditions.

Determining adequate fee structures for advisors

Typically, the compensation structure has been linked to the size of transaction. The remuneration of the advisors will depend on the nature and extent of the advisory task. A fixed fee is commonplace as well as a percentage of the value of the shares sold, for what concerns financial advisors. Fees have can also be structured based on performance of advisors (e.g. in share allocation or if privatisation proceeds exceed certain predefined minima). Other advisors such as legal and auditing firms are normally paid either their standard fees (often hourly) or a specially negotiated one-off remuneration for their services.

Of particular controversy is the advisory fee for investment banking which can be based on a percentage of the transaction. For an auction the investment bank may charge a fee lower than 1 per cent. For IPOs the "floor price" can range between 1.5 to 2 per cent of the total amount sold, but that is often because banks will underwrite the transaction and need to be compensated for risk. However, caution should be exercised to avoid excessive fees. This underscores the importance of a reliable valuation of the SOE to be privatised, because if the fee structure is designed to reward a "successful" sale even at a comparably low price then the financial advisor's incentives may become misaligned with those of the government. It also raises specific challenges regarding the structuring in incentives in the case where the government's privatisation objectives may not be solely based on maximising the proceeds.

Often fees are negotiable and it is reported that advisors may accept lower fees when working with the government as it apparently helps to build their credibility with other clients.

Box 4.3. Special section on dealing with external advisors

Separation of strategic from transaction-specific advisory mandates

The separation of advisory and sale mandates helps reduce the likelihood of conflicts of interest. The advisory mandate can help to determine the best sales strategy and timeline; and the sales mandate can execute the transaction. By ensuring a separation between the two the government can enhance the independence of the advice and the best outcome for the sale based on the objectives it has set out.

Separation of government shareholder's advisors from the SOE's advisors

When the government and the SOEs have the same company advising them on legal or financial issues the likelihood of the advice being compromised is increased. In such cases it is best if the company and the government have separate advisors. However, common advice in areas such as presentational or marketing strategy might be beneficial.

Open and transparent competitive processes should be used for hiring advisors

In order to ensure best value and to protect the transparency of the privatisation process governments should hire advisors through a competitive bidding process. But in light of the importance of technical specialised skills, it is important to ensure that competitive processes assign sufficient weight to the quality, competence, and experience of advisors as the key criteria in the selection. In this regard it would be useful to develop a list of qualified bidders (by establishing lists or framework agreements) instead of focusing exclusively on cost.

Ensure that the advisor is only representing the government or its selling agent's interests

The government needs to ensure that the advisor is not working for (or is not indirectly related to the potential bidders, and that the information obtained by the advisor does not make its way to potential bidders.

Ensure that the pay structure does not create incentives for working against the government interests

Commissions should be carefully calibrated to avoid any bias in favour of options that are against government objectives, e.g. granting monopoly rights in order to generate bigger commissions from the sale. As noted above, acquiring the best advice plays a very important part in ensuring the success of privatisation.

Source: Adaptation from OECD (2009).

Figure 4.2. Integrity of the privatisation process: dealing with external advisors

A few areas deserve particular attention to ensure that working with external advisors does not compromise the integrity of the privatisation process.

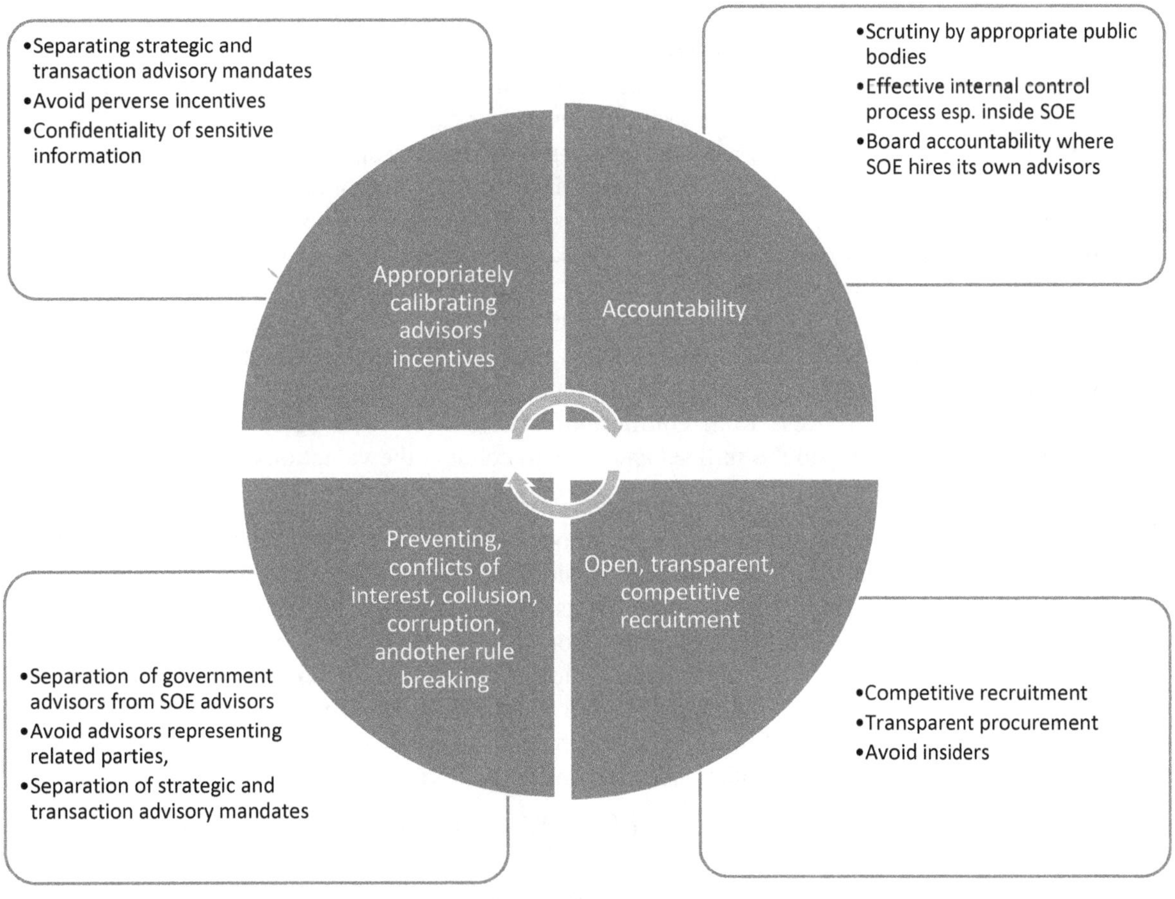

Determining company valuation and establishing sound pricing methods

Even if the key objective of privatisation is not solely revenue maximisation, one of the measures of success post-privatisation will be the value of the transaction and ensuring that the asset was sold for "fair market value". An appropriate valuation method will ensure that the state can justify its pricing of shares, to assure both a fair price, value for money and to attract sufficient interest from investors. Ultimately, the government has a fiduciary duty towards citizens to ensure to sell assets at a fair market value[2]. However, sometimes the government may decide to sell at below market value for policy reasons - for example selling shares to employees at a discount; or attracting foreign direct investment which may result in technology transfers, spill overs and other backward linkages which may be part of policy objectives. Where these specific reasons exist, they should be clearly identified and made transparent to avoid viewing the sale as favouring a certain buyer. The valuation process is also an important aspect to determine the choice of sales methods – or in the case of public offerings, sequencing – may depend on the valuation of the company in alternative scenarios, as may the ultimate decision whether to privatise now or postpone the transaction. Moreover, specific decisions in the privatisation process such as share allocations (in the case of public offerings), incentive fee structures to external advisors, ex-post evaluations of the outcome of privatisation as well as, ultimately, the propriety of the process itself may all hinge on a benchmark established up front. Even in the case of listed SOEs where a market valuation already exists many governments wish to consider the likely impact of further privatisation on corporate value. In a small number of countries (including France, Italy, Poland, Spain and Turkey) valuation prior to privatisation is even mandated by law. It can be considered best practice that valuation is conducted on a regular (possibly annual) basis, especially in the few years leading up to the sale. This is especially important in wholly-owned companies to ensure that the ownership entity is confident in advising decision-makers on the potential value of assets that are slated for privatisation (and in general for determining the value of the state portfolio). In a large majority of OECD countries valuation is undertaken by independent external advisors. Conversely, a few countries have followed a different road, leaving the valuation task to a specialist commission within the government (e.g. France, Korea, and Turkey). This method is intended to shield the valuation process from conflicts of interests. In other cases, the ownership entity may have developed the skill set and tools to conduct the valuations in-house.

The issue of valuation is rather controversial in that it requires a certain degree of subjectivity, not only in terms of the method chosen (see non-exhaustive overview below), but also in terms of the political decision making that must accompany it. In an auction, the potential buyer will also conduct its own valuation, based on a different set of criteria and assumptions, for example based on its assessment of developing synergies between its business and the potential acquisition. According to the German privatisation experience, the valuation should be reasonable and fair in terms of the status of the asset and market realities; and if it does meet the objectives for the sale, the shareholder may consider further restructuring, other sales options, or postponing the sale.

The valuation process will build upon a financial audit and determining the method of sale (see Chapter 3 for more on methods of sale). The financial audit of the company's accounts is necessary to complete the valuation methodology, and it will play a key factor in determine the method of sale. For conglomerates, there should be an analysis of the valuation for each business segment or division.

In parallel to the audit, due diligence will need to be conducted, which consists of gathering and verifying information on the financing of the company, its balance sheet, international standing (as applicable), and other information relevant to the valuation, such as changes in taxation or regulation (e.g. legal, accounting, strategic, environmental, tax, etc.). Past financial performance and projections on future earnings and investments are examined. All this information is essential to determine the valuation (see also Chapter 3 on pre-privatisation company restructuring). It is also worth pointing out that some businesses are valued according to their absolute value and others according to their relative value (e.g. financial institutions or utilities are commonly valued in a particular way). The below table provides a non-exhaustive overview of methods, but it should be noted that the choice of methodology will be asset-dependent.

Table 4.1. Examples of valuation methodologies

Valuation methods are based on an estimate of market value, but require some level of interpretation and subjectivity. The below table provides a non-exhaustive overview of methods, but it should be noted that the choice of methodology will often be asset-dependent.

Valuation method	Description	Pros	Cons	Privatisation method
Discounted cash-flow	Estimation of the company's free cash flows over a medium to long-term horizon, taking into account variations in working capital and future capital expenditures. A discount rate is applied to future cash flow to represent present value. Discount value is based on the weighted average cost of capital and political risk. Debt is subtracted to arrive at net present value of company's equity.	Comparable with other companies; complex model can help to anticipate arguments or concerns raised by potential buyers.	Requires an extensive model, with a number of variables of varying degree of sensitivity.	Strategic investor, public offering
Comparable companies or "trading multiples analysis"	Apply derived valuation multiples to latest financial results and compare them across companies/transactions. Multiples include: turnover, operating income (EBITA or EBIT), net earnings (price-earnings ratio).	Useful estimate of market value based on public information	Valuation multiples require interpretation, subjectivity, small number of comparable peer firms	Public offering
Comparable transactions or " "precedent transactions analysis"	Determines the multiples paid in the past for acquisitions of similar companies. Places value of in a change of control situation.	Based on public information, gauge of investor appetite and market demand, range of plausible premiums	Valuation multiples require interpretation, no transaction is alike, public data limited, sensitive to market fluctuations	
Adjusted net assets	Estimates the market value of assets (fixed and current) and then subtracts its balance sheet and off balance sheet liabilities.	Seller can prefer to determine selling price to "get money back" after depreciation	Does not take into account to future cash flows. Buyers do not like.	Strategic investor
Replacement value method	Estimate of cost to replace company's assets if destroyed. Includes fixed assets, start-up costs and current assets.	Useful to anticipate arguments or concerns raised if critics claim an asset is undersold.	Higher valuation than other methods, Buyers do not like. Does not take into account expected return	
Combination of methods	When company groups are complex, different lines of business can be estimated separately based on price earnings multiples, discounted cash flows or other methods.			

Source: World Bank and Author.

Another important consideration is whether the government should set a "reservation price" or a "minimum price". Although systematic processes are not very common some jurisdictions have established a special commission or other special bodies responsible to oversee this process. For example, in France an independent commission named the Shareholdings and Transfers Commission (see also reference to this body in earlier sections) can be seized under particular circumstances. This Commission must give an assent to the privatization operations, particularly on the sale price and, if applicable, on the privatization procedure implemented. An evaluation of the privatized enterprise is carried out by the Commission and the transfer price cannot be less than the one suggested by the assessment (see Box 4.4). In other cases, budget laws may set out clear objectives for the government to see for the “best price.”

All valuation methods are established based on an estimate of market value. No one method is infallible, and will depend on the method of privatisation; it is further complicated by the fact that there is often no comparable entity operating in the same market to allow for a peer-based evaluation. As such different methods can be used for company valuation and depending on the jurisdiction may also be prescribed by the enacting privatisation legislation. The method employed will also be asset-dependent. The most common methods are the discounted cash flow method, and the comparable transaction or companies methods. Other methods also exist, including the adjusted net assets method or replacement value method. These are further described in Table 4.1.

No matter the method established, the valuation process is considered to be an important factor in evaluating the success of the transaction, and in determining *ex-post* whether the objectives and rationales set (and ideally communicated) at the outset of the process have been met (see also Chapter 5). As mentioned, the government should have clearly stated sales objectives at the outset of the process. In most cases these will be “financial objectives” with value maximisation and obtaining the “best price” being key factors. It is worth noting that some cases “non-financial” objectives, such as attracting foreign direct investment or capital markets development, may be considered equally as important as value maximisation and should also factor into the government’s decision-making process. Should this be the case, these objectives should be rationalised and transparently communicated at the start of the process.

Box 4.4. Valuation methods: Case example from France

The French Shareholdings and Transfers Commission’s most important task is to value SOEs with a view to ensuring that publicly-owned assets are sold at a fair price in accordance with legal provisions.

The Commission conduct an analysis using "commonly employed” methods based on “multiple criteria” including existing the market capitalisation, revalued consolidated net assets, profitability and “future prospects”.

The Commission has valuation reports drawn up by the government’s advising banks and the advising bank(s) for the company to be sold (or the report from the independent expert appointed by the seller in the case of secondary sales of subsidiaries belonging to public entities). These reports provide valuation brackets derived from the different applicable methods. They generally propose estimates based on:

- the market capitalisation (spot price on a given date or average over a certain period deemed significant)
- revalued consolidated net assets
- a peer-based comparison, or comparison with similar transactions: the price earnings multiples observed in the sector are applied to the forecasts for the company's key multiples (mainly EBITDA and price/earnings ratio and more rarely turnover)
- discounted cash flows or dividends.

When the group is complex, its different lines of business can be estimated separately based on price earnings multiples, discounted cash flows or more sophisticated methods.

For listed companies, the operation carried out by the government must comply with market integrity rules. The opinion of financial analysts employed by major institutions that follow the stock, particularly if it is listed, may also be taken into account along with the target price, if there is one.

The Commission assesses the results of the different approaches and discusses them at hearings with the Government Shareholdings Agency (APE), the company whose shares are sold and the advising banks. It requests any additional information required to examine the dossier (extent and duration of guarantees, any remaining public sector expenses and tax and labour legislation concerns). If necessary, the Commission may ask for other business case scenarios to be assessed. After deliberation, it sets the value of the company as required by law, or, where applicable, issues an opinion on the exchange parity.

Source: Commission des Participations et des Transferts (2016).

Determining potential buyers and handling bids

Establishing criteria and conducting due diligence for potential buyers

It is fairly common for countries to establish criteria for potential buyers and conducting due diligence. This may apply only to specific types of transactions (i.e. private sale). In general most countries impose criteria on potential bidders to ensure that the buyers/management possess the financial and technical capacity to run the business successfully; to ensure their credibility; and, future solvency.

In some cases, restrictions may apply to the nationality or type of company involved in the acquisition if there are specific restrictions related to national security or public interest where these assets are deemed to be "strategic". For example in Poland, the *2016 on the principles of state property management* (article 13) introduces a total ban on selling shares of 24 pre-identified companies which are mainly of a strategic nature. As laid out in the *2009 OECD Guidelines for Recipient Country Investment Policies Relating to National Security* (OECD, 2009a), these practices should be made transparent and limited to ensure that they are not used as disguised protectionism.[3] Moreover, as highlighted in the *OECD Guidelines on Corporate Governance of State-Owned Enterprises* ("OECD SOE Guidelines") such types of control mechanisms should only be used when they are strictly necessary to protect certain essential public interests such as those relating to the protection of public security and proportionate to the pursuit of these objectives.

In other cases, and as consisted with the stated "immaterial" goals that are defined as part of the sales objectives domestic (retail) investors may be among targeted buyers. In these cases, such objectives should be clearly defined upfront, and perhaps subject to quotas to ensure they are not unduly restrictive. For example, in New Zealand, for companies privatised under its "mixed ownership" programme, the government had placed a quota on the total per cent shares reserved for domestic investors in an energy company offering.

Authorities need to consider carefully alternative legal or regulatory measures that may be more appropriate to directly targeting investors. It is often more efficient to work through pre-qualification following by bidding among the selected candidates than allowing the targeting to interfere with the selection of individual buyers. Full disclosure should be made, to minority shareholders as well as the general public, of the criteria according to which a preference for certain shareholders is developed and the objectives they are expected to pursue following privatisation. Care should also be taken to ensure that the pricing of trade sales is not so conservative as to raise concerns – especially where this is subject to specific laws or EU regulation – about state subsidisation of the buyers. Throughout the process, the entity steering the transaction should carefully manage confidentiality and transparency requirements of the sale.

Table 4.2. Determining criteria for buyers: Using due diligence or other appropriate mechanisms

National security Public interest	• Maintaining majority ownership, golden shares, high-vote shares • Separating out sensitive assets prior to sale • Establishing restrictions through bylaws or charters • Specifying non-pecuniary objectives beforehand • Transparent investment policy if restrictions on foreign ownership
Ethics track record of buyer	• Due diligence • Requirement to adhere to international agreements
Solvency of buyer, technical capacity	• Due diligence • Requirement for bank guarantees by buyer
Targeting investors	• Quotas on % of shares reserved for domestic investors • Clawback clauses to increase quantity of shares offered to retail investors • Offering shares to retail investors at a discount • Quotas on % of shares reserved for employees

Above and beyond the criteria described above, relatively few countries have established procedures to carry out due diligence on potential buyers based on their ethics track record. In Sweden, for example, bidders have to fill out a Corporate Conduct and Compliance Questionnaire. The assessment criteria relate to tax structures, corruption, money laundering, and other illegal asset transfers, environmental and labour practices and more serious violations of international law including in the area of terrorism and human rights violations aiming at identifying any history of corporate law breaking. The questionnaire not only considers the buyer's track record, but also those of associated companies, as well as members of the board and senior management (Box 4.5).

Box 4.5. Due diligence on potential buyers based on their ethics track record: Case example from Sweden

The Swedish government has set high expectations that state-owned companies act as role models in the area of "sustainable business" (as defined according to UN and OECD backed standards of corporate ethics) and, moreover, acts in a way that they ensure public confidence. In addition, due to Swedish obligations under international treaties the government has set some basic requirements for purchasers of state assets as far as ethical conduct is concerned.

These requirements are reflected in a "Conduct and Compliance Questionnaire", which contain assessment criteria intended to be applied to the sale of shares in non-listed companies with state ownership. The assessment criteria relate to tax structures, corruption, money laundering, and other illegal asset transfers, environmental and labour practices and more serious violations of international law including in the area of terrorism and human rights violations. The questionnaire not only considers the buyer's track record, but also those of associated companies, as well as members of the board and senior management. It covers some of the following areas:

- Violation, or previous violations of Swedish tax law or transfer of tax base of company to a jurisdiction with a low tax base (i.e. tax base of less than 10%)
- Tax fraud or tax evasion of members of the board of directors or senior management
- Buyer or any associated companies, members of the board of directors or senior management committed violations against the law and regulations against foreign bribery; terrorist financing; or any other form of illegal transfers
- Buyer or any associated companies, members of the board of directors or senior management violations of international law (incl. genocide, war crimes, crimes against humanity; or serious or systematic violations against human rights:
- Buyer or any associated companies' violations of labour legislation, international labour standards and the OECD MNE Guidelines; and,
- Buyer or any associated companies' violations of environmental legislation.

The questionnaire allows the government to consider the response provided by the bidders to the criteria set out above when evaluating the bids provided in a sale process within the framework of the budget law's business requirements.

Source: Submission by Swedish authorities.

Handling bids transparently

It is important to establish adequate and transparent procedures for bid handling, which don't violate the confidentiality terms of the sale, to avoid irregular practices and ensure that bidders that consider that their rights have been violated have access to recourse. In general, where specific qualifications for bidders are being sought this must be made transparent in advance (see also above). The main options available to governments include specifying non-pecuniary objectives beforehand and conducting the bidding with these as a sub-condition; and relying on a formal or informal prequalification of bidders (Figure 4.3).

Figure 4.3. Process involved with buyers in a trade sale

An auction and negotiated sale involve different levels of interaction with the potential buyer(s).

Source: World Bank.

Prospectus

External financial advisors of the sales agent will draft the prospectus in cooperation with government officials as well as the SOE executive management. The prospectus must address information on the business, and detailed information on the financials and risks of the company. It will also cover the dividend policy, environmental issues, regulatory regime, employee and management participation to the sale (if applicable), management or other government residual shareholders (if applicable) and the government intentions towards the company and industry. What goes into the prospectus will differ across jurisdictions as per legal requirements and listing requirements of different exchanges.[4]

Figure 4.4. Public offering process

The public offering process will involve various levels of interaction between the investment bank executing the offer and the government/SOE.

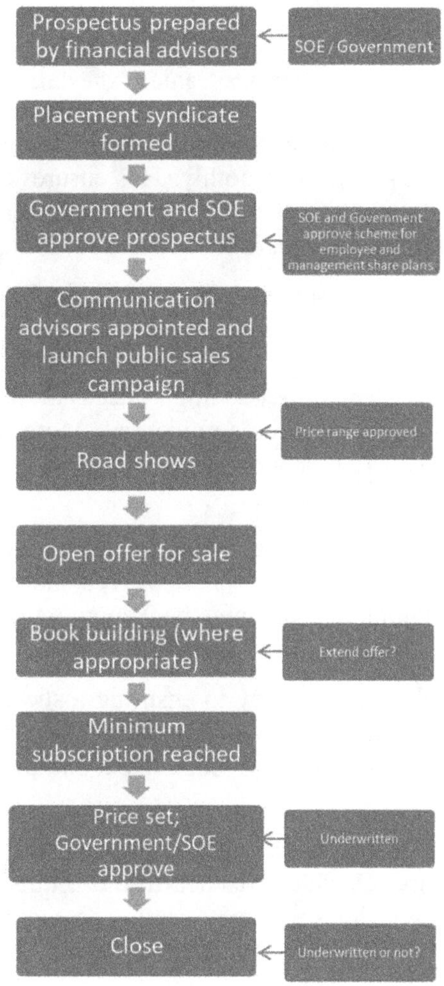

Source: Adapted from PwC (2013).

Confidential exchange of information with buyers

For a trade sale the standard procedure first includes establishing a long-list of buyers, who are then subject to a confidentiality agreement. The seller will then share partial information about the sale in the form of a "sales book" or "information memorandum". Based on this information, potential buyers make an indicative offer on the basis of which the shortlist is drawn up. The shortlisted bidders gain access to the data room (virtual data rooms are more common today) where they can consult very detailed information about the company and, on the basis of this and other information, perform due diligence (See Box 4.6). Following this, binding offers are submitted to the bank for eventual review by the ownership unit and, if this is mandated by national rules, shared with the higher levels of government. During this phase, careful balance is needed to respect strict confidentiality requirements required by the sale, with the need for high transparency.

The trade sales process does in some countries involve setting a minimum price, the existence of which will in this case be communicated to the bidders beforehand. The seller will balance the need to be transparent but also ensure that the sale is subject to confidentiality to avoid any risks to the transaction. For this reason, in a negotiated sale the exchange of confidential information can occur through either an information memorandum or through a secure data room.

Box 4.6. Value of the data room

The government shareholder needs to work with the company management to ensure that the preparation of the sale goes smoothly. This ensures compiling a full set of information that needs to go into the data room. A lack of documentation or incomplete information can lead to a sale falling through, or that buyers set forth certain conditions on the sale.

The data room is an important place to share information with potential buyers concerning the contracts, intellectual property information, employee information, financial statements, capitalisation, and more. The seller can allow for access to key information that a potential buyer might need to follow-through with a bid, while ensuring that information remains confidential. More recently privatisation transactions have moved towards online data rooms, as opposed to physical data rooms, and this has helped to speed up transactions.

The online data room can be established to allow access to all documents or only to a subset of documents, and only to pre-approved individuals. A number of online data rooms allow the seller or its investment bankers to review who has been in the data room, how often that party has been in the data room, and the dates of entry into the data room.

A compete online data room is key to ensuring a successful transaction. The number of documents that need to be provided on the company and its subsidiaries is rather extensive. As such, adequate time should be put into compiling the list of required documentation.

The online data room should be prepared in conjunction with preparation of the selling company's disclosure schedules attached to the acquisition agreement, as complete and accurate disclosure schedules are key to getting an acquisition completed.

Source: Harroch (2016).

Active and on-going communication

To ensure the smooth execution of the transaction, active and on-going communication with stakeholders and the public is important. Of course the government communication's strategy will differ according to the asset and mode of sale. A communication plan can cover: communication with other parts of government and parliament; as well as communication with the board, management and employees' representatives during the privatisation process. Where stakeholders or particular communities are affected by the transaction, it is suggested to have a proactive communication plan as well as risk mitigation strategy - especially if the transaction is not popular. Finally, an on-going public communication strategy will be necessary to inform the general public on progress and in the event of the finalisation of the transaction.

Importantly a communication strategy will be important to develop an appetite for potential buyers - the latter is often developed with an external advisor. This means developing professional management presentations that can be delivered as part of the roadshow before a sale.

Notes

[1] Further information regarding this point and exemptions in public procurement rules will be requested.

[2] In the case of an IPO, one could go a step further with this logic to say that there is also a duty to ensure fair market value for small retail investors.

[3] It should be observed that some governments retain golden shares which provide them with special powers and veto rights in fully or partially privatised companies. In some cases these mechanisms have served governments as a means of protecting the newly privatised company from hostile takeovers on national security or on public policy grounds, where this has been deemed to be necessary. According to OECD SOE Guideline IV.A.1, the use of golden shares should be limited to cases where they are strictly necessary to protect certain essential public interests such as those relating to the protection of public security and proportionate to the pursuit of these objectives. Further, governments should disclose the existence of any shareholders' agreements and capital structures that allow a shareholder to exercise a degree of control over the corporation disproportionate to the shareholders' equity ownership in the enterprise. This is covered in more detail in Chapter 5.

[4] It is noteworthy to mention that the EU Prospectus Regulation, which will apply from July 2019 (with some limited exceptions) and will be directly effective in Member State aims to harmonise disclosure across the EU and allows for the establishment of a cross-border passport mechanism which facilitates the effective functioning of the internal market in a wide variety of securities. It has provisions directly imposing obligations on persons involved in offers of securities to the public and in admissions of securities to trading on a regulated market which are applied in a uniform manner throughout the Union (European Commission, 2017).

References

European Commission (2017), "Prospectus - Regulation (EU) 2017/1129".

Harroch R. (2016), "The Importance of Online Data Rooms in Mergers and Acquisitions", Forbes.com.

OECD (2015), *OECD Guidelines on Corporate Governance of State-Owned Enterprises*, 2015 Edition, http://dx.doi.org/10.1787/9789264244160-en.

OECD (2010), *Privatisation in the 21st Century: Summary of Recent Experiences*, https://www.oecd.org/daf/ca/corporategovernanceofstate-ownedenterprises/43449100.pdf.

OECD (2009a), OECD Guidelines for Recipient Country Investment Policies Relating to National Security, Paris, https://www.oecd.org/daf/inv/investment-policy/43384486.pdf.

OECD (2009b), *Privatisation in the 21st Century: Recent Experiences of OECD Countries: Report on Good Practices*, January 2009, https://www.oecd.org/daf/ca/corporategovernanceofstate-ownedenterprises/48476423.pdf.

OECD (2003), *Privatising State-Owned Enterprises: An Overview of Policies and Practices in OECD Countries*, OECD Publishing, Paris, https://doi.org/10.1787/9789264104099-en.

PriceWaterhouseCoopers (PwC) (2013)," A beginner's guide to privatisations", PriceWaterhouseCoopers in Cyprus.

World Bank (1997), "The Privatisation Challenge: A strategic, legal, and institutional analysis of international experience", World Bank Publishing.

World Bank (1998), "The Case-bv-Case Approach to Privatization: Techniques and Examples", World Bank Publishing.

Chapter 5. Steps to be taken post-privatisation

The work on privatisation should not be seen terminated upon finalisation of the divestment process. This chapter discusses steps to be taken post-privatisation including in regard to ensuring any residual guarantees are budgeted and any contingent liabilities assessed; transparency and accountability in the use of the privatisation proceeds; assessing the outcomes of privatisation, including auditing the transaction; and, good governance practices in the case of partial privatisation.

The work on privatisation should not be seen as terminated upon finalisation of the divestment process. This chapter discusses steps that need to be taken post-privatisation, including in regard to ensuring any residual guarantees are budgeted and any contingent liabilities assessed; transparency and accountability in the use of the privatisation proceeds; assessing the outcomes of privatisation, including auditing the transaction; and, taking steps to ensure good governance of partly privatised entities.

Handling residual guarantees or liabilities

Most legal systems regulate the transfer of debts and obligations including contingent liabilities (e.g. derived from ongoing or potential litigation). In civil law countries, debt transfers are subject to the creditor's approval, without which the original debtor continues to be liable. In the case of a privatisation, that situation is not altered. However, if the state-owned enterprise's (SOE's) legal status is changed through corporatisation, then the creditor may not be satisfied with the new status of an implicit backing by the state, especially where a limited liability company organized under company law may reduce the security afforded to its creditors to the amount of the new company's declared capital. This is why the framework or privatisation legislation would normally specify how the public authority involved in executing the transaction should defray costs, including debt write-offs resulting from balance sheet adjustments. Normally this would also be taken care of in the pre-privatisation restructuring of the company.

Accountability and transparency in handling privatisation proceeds

As discussed in Chapter 2, the rationales for privatisation should be clear before embarking on the transaction and so too should the use for privatisation proceeds. These can be used to fund various policy priorities. Whatever the end use, there should be a high level of accountability and transparency in handling the proceeds especially if they are (eventually) diverted to achieve certain public policy goals (e.g. reduce debt, reinvestment of proceeds to support public services or other policy priorities, etc.).

The state can receive privatisation proceeds in different ways, and they can either be used immediately or earmarked for a limited time for a specific purpose. The legal decision triggering the sell-off (either in the context of a privatisation framework or transaction-related legislation) should specify the use of the privatisation proceeds and should clarify how the funds should be used, for example (Seven, 2002):

- *General government revenue.* Allocated to treasury as public revenue and subject to public finance laws (with or without constraints on how it is used) and subject to parliamentary authorisation and scrutiny.
- *Proceeds allocated or earmarked to a special purpose fund.* This could be a sovereign wealth fund, pensions fund, innovation fund or another type of special purpose fund. The funds can have the purpose of financing a number of public interest priorities for example pension liabilities of privatised companies; to finance infrastructure projects; or develop a fund for innovative start-ups). If allocated to a special fund a separate set of laws will determine how the fund is set-up, operated or monitored.
- *Funding of privatisation transaction.* Sales proceeds are also often used to pay for expenditures required to execute the privatisation process, redundancy payments, loan write-offs, payment of advisors, etc., which would also be subject to parliamentary authorisation and scrutiny, but covered by the privatisation

legislation. These are often funded by the public budget in a specialised privatisation account.

- *A mix of uses.* In some cases part of the revenue may go into the general government fund with the funds earmarked for a special purpose (e.g. social security payments, pension liabilities, funding adjustment policies for affected employees, to purchase shares in another enterprise; to purchase government bonds).

In the cases involving the sale of assets (e.g. a division, factory or subsidiary) the process may be more complicated as under company law (and under public enterprise laws where they exist) the proceeds may revert to the seller. In this case, the seller would often be the company itself, and the use of proceeds would be subject to the decision of the board of directors. Where the state is the sole or majority shareholder the state is in a positon to recover the proceeds through its dividends policy.

The privatisation legislation should provide rules on the method of payment expected from the private investor. Cash payments are preferred, but may also involve special financing techniques such as deferred payment (seller financing) or credit (bank financing). Where shares are paid in instalments the voting power of shareholders who have not paid the full amount of their shares can be limited and their shares held in escrow accounts until the last instalments have been paid (Seven, 2002).

Systematically conducting post-privatisation evaluation

Good practice calls for the competent authorities to conduct an independent evaluation of the past privatisation projects undertaken. This should be based on the criteria set out at the beginning of the process, in terms of achieving the stated goals, rationales and objectives. A post-privatisation evaluation should also include an assessment of corporate efficiency, effects on markets and stakeholders. Finally, good policy practice would encourage independent evaluation of the impact of the privatisation in terms of consumers, especially where public service delivery is concerned. These are most often performed by the national audit office (see also below).

In some jurisdictions post-privatisation evaluations can also be conducted by a specific commission with a mandate to supervise and assess the privatisation transaction; by the Ministry of Finance in the context of annual policy evaluation; by parliamentary inquiry[1]; the ownership or privatisation agency. For example:

- In France, this is done by the Shareholdings and Transfers Commission which is responsible for supervising and assessing the privatization operations. The results of its inquiry are made public at the end of each transaction.
- In Japan in the cases of recent stock offerings of JT, NTT, JP, and Kyushu Railway Company, the outcomes of privatisation are subject to assessment in the annual Policy Evaluation Reports of the Ministry of Finance.
- In Turkey, the Privatisation Administration includes a Post Privatisation Department, which exercises post-privatisation oversight of fully divested enterprises. The Department monitors whether parties to past privatisations fulfil their obligations (and are granted their rights) under the contracts and agreements entered as part of the divestment. The Department further monitors the privatised enterprises with respect to such criteria as profitability, employment and investment. It carries out studies and assessments with the purpose of providing proposals concerning future privatisations.

- In the Netherlands, the Senate has performed a parliamentary enquiry of the Dutch privatisation practices (See also Box 5.1).

Policy makers should be held equally accountable for the outcomes of the privatisation process and ensuring that the transaction was carried out in the best interest of the public. Appropriate recourse mechanisms should be made available in the case of non-fulfilment of obligations by the buyer following privatisation; or if the transaction was subject to irregular practices.

Box 5.1. Post-privatisation evaluation: Case study from the Netherlands

Post-privatisation evaluation in the Netherlands is performed by Parliament as part of regulatory parliamentary inquiry; in 2012 it conducted an inquiry to evaluate privatisation transactions that took place over two decades from 1990 to 2010. A summary of the elements of this report is provided as an example of national practice.

The Netherlands parliament examined privatisation transactions taken place from 1990-2010 to evaluate the way privatisation was orchestrated, its institutional framework as well as how stakeholders were involved in the broader public and parliamentary debate. The report offered recommendations on how to improve the process in the future. It determined that:

- *Complex institutional environment.* Privatisation transactions were carried out in a complex and changing environment and that there was no coordination of policies, no common road map but there were many differences in the implementation of decisions by ministries. There were no broadly accepted frameworks for decision-making to ensure coherent policy-making. As a result, decision-making about privatization took up a lot of time and attention in parliament. The committee determined that the national government should create more uniformity in how decisions about privatization are implemented. A well-defined structure is needed to achieve more clarity about the different public and private forms of policy execution. This calls for a government wide approach, to be coordinated.
- *A new role for parliament.* The committee concluded that the parliament has to rethink how it should fulfil its various law-making, control and representation roles. In particular, it determined that the authority of parliament should be very clear however, both in terms of its role as legislature and controller. This requires comprehensive legal frameworks, to assess and support decision-making. This could be achieved by strengthening the roles of legislature and controller, while taking into account that the public sector has become more complex.
- *Effects for citizens and public interest.* The committee concluded that by focusing on the roles of citizens as client and tax payer, a too narrow perspective on public interests was used, and that particularly fuelled the public's dissatisfaction with privatization. Therefore, it was concluded that a broader perspective needs to be developed and applied to look at both interests of individual citizens as well as collective interests that benefit all.
- *Parliamentary control.* The committee determined that it could exert its control function where incomplete decisions had led to unsatisfactory outcomes or suboptimal governance arrangements. As a result, it concluded that Parliament should develop new instruments and ways to reinforce its control on policy execution at arm's length.

In response to these recommendations the government has agreed to use the decision framework developed by the parliamentary inquiry committee if it intends to privatize a SOE. The decision framework consists of five steps: (1) intention, (2) design, (3) decision, (4) execution, (5) follow-up. By following the five steps in this context, the parliament is informed timely and adequately about decisions about privatization.

Source: Eerste Kamer der Staten-Generaal (2012).

Subjecting the transaction to an ex-post audit process

As a separate element of the post-privatisation evaluation, in most countries, privatisation is subject to an audit process, either during or after privatisation. In some cases this is done through an internal audit process in the responsible ministries and, in a few countries, governmental committees overseeing the privatisation process. Countries differ with respect to whether the state auditors may only carry out ex-post auditing or are empowered to intervene during the privatisation process itself. The state auditor's core roles include carrying out an audit of past privatisations with a view to assess propriety and value for money, and the achievement of other goals and objectives set out as part of the sales objectives (e.g. transfer of future liabilities; absence of future government funding, assessment of efficiency gains realised by the private sector). The latter involves comparing privatisation revenues with pre-privatisation valuation and may extend to an assessment of the valuation methodology. It will also need to take into consideration information available at the time of the transaction; and the achievement of immaterial goals identified at the outset of the process.

Box 5.2. Ex-post audit of a privatisation transaction: Case examples from the UK

Royal Mail

In October 2013, the Shareholder Executive managed the sale of a 60 per cent stake in the UK government's shareholding in Royal Mail through an initial public offering. Following the sale, the National Audit Office (NAO) evaluated the transaction to examine whether the Shareholder Executive achieved the UK government's sale objectives, while protecting the taxpayers' interests. Moreover, a secondly inquiry by the Public Accounts Committee (a cross-party parliamentary body) reviewed the transaction and drew up its own conclusions.

The NAO ex-post audit covered the following areas:

- the context for the sale
- restructuring Royal Mail's business in readiness for sale
- advisers, transaction alternatives and valuation
- book-building, final demand and pricing.

In the UK typically the Public Accounts Committee (a cross-party parliamentary body) will also review the transaction drawing on the National Audit Office report and then producing its own report on the success or otherwise of the privatisation.

Lloyd's Banking Group

Between September 2013 and May 2017, UK Financial Investments (UKFI; now incorporated under UK Government Investments, a company wholly owned by HM Treasury) managed the sale of the government's 43 per cent shareholding in Lloyds Banking Group, acquired through measures to maintain financial stability in 2008-09. Following the sale, the National Audit Office (NAO) conducted a review of the process, focusing on what Government could learn from its experience in the Lloyds sale with a view to applying this to future transactions – particularly the sale of the government's remaining holding in Royal Bank of Scotland.

Although the review did not form a judgement on the value for money of the share sales, the NAO's review of the process as a whole was positive. They found UKFI and its advisers to have prepared for, and executed, the transactions professionally and in cash terms the sale returned the taxpayers' original investment. The NAO's published report outlined observations and recommendations for future sales, focusing on three aspects: sale preparation, sale execution, and sale outcome.

Source: National Audit Office, 2014 and 2018.

Good governance practices in the case of partial privatisation

This section will briefly discuss best practices in terms of government ownership practices in the case of a partial privatisation. In particular, if the state still effectively controls the company, controls are needed to ensure an adequate protection of minority shareholders.

"Golden" shares

"Golden" shares provide governments with special powers and veto rights in the fully or partially privatised companies, and have served governments as a means of protecting the newly privatised company from hostile takeovers on national security or on public policy grounds, where this has been deemed to be necessary. "Golden" shares have been widely adopted and introduced across numerous OECD and OECD Partner countries, and have often served as a key element of post-privatisation control devices. At the same time, in the European Union, countries have tread cautiously with regard to retaining golden shares to avoid violating rules relating to the free movement of capital, as upheld by numerous judgements of the European Court of Justice.

According to the *OECD Guidelines on Corporate Governance of State-Owned Enterprises* ("OECD SOE Guidelines"), the use of "golden" shares should be limited to cases where they are strictly necessary to protect certain essential public interests such as those relating to the protection of public security and proportionate to the pursuit of these objectives (Figure 5.1). Further, governments should disclose the existence of any shareholders' agreements and capital structures that allow a shareholder to exercise a degree of control over the corporation disproportionate to the shareholders' equity ownership in the enterprise.

"Golden" shares can have some drawbacks in the sense that the potential for government intervention is greater, thus creating more investor uncertainty. The degree to which "golden" shares have proven to be detrimental to the spirit of privatisation is largely influenced by the breadth of their scope, their duration, and the extent to which the government has exercised the powers afforded to it by the "golden" share. In the absence of an effective regulatory capacity (e.g. where the institutions and the market need time to develop), and in the case of companies where there are specific national interests are at stake, golden shares can help facilitate privatisation and are arguably better than establishing a standard policy of limiting foreign ownership and control by legislation.

Figure 5.1. Golden rules about "Golden" shares

Golden shares can be used by government owners as a post-privatisation control device, however according to the OECD SOE Guidelines some important "golden rules" should apply.

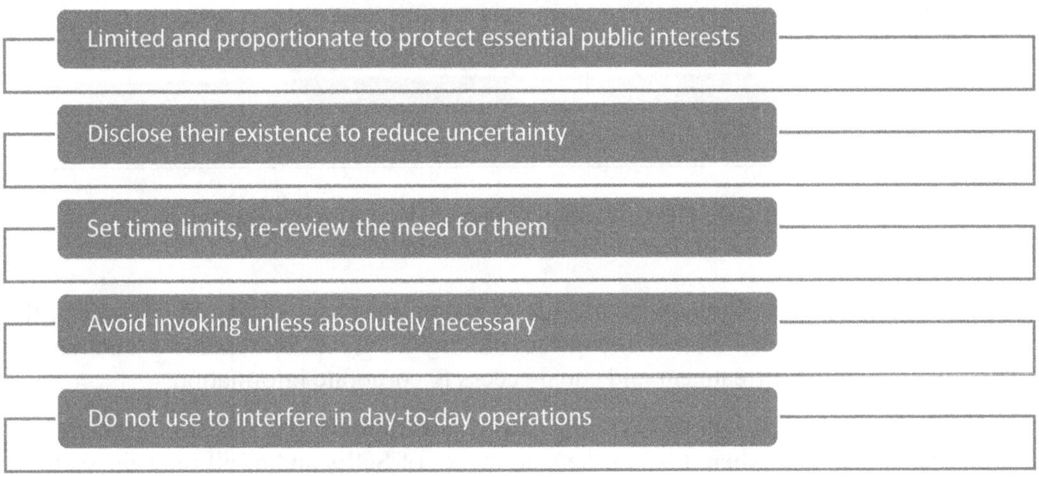

Source: OECD (2015) and OECD (2003).

Protecting minority shareholders and stakeholders

The presence of non-State minority shareholders is important, as it allows outside investors to participate in the shareholders' meetings and in some cases have a deciding vote in areas where the government as a controlling shareholder is conflicted. However, it might be appropriate for the State as an owner to reassure minority shareholders that their interests are taken into consideration (Box 5.3). Particular concerns may arise where the State must balance the control of the SOE where (majority) public interests remain, while ensuring the protection of minority shareholders. The role of minorities may differ in the case of an initial public offering versus for an unlisted business. In all case the protections for minority shareholders should be as laid down in the relevant legislation and/or listing requirements (See Figure 5.2).

Empirical research suggests that shareholder rights protection is positively related to performance improvements following listing. Where the State remains the controlling shareholder its identity and intentions matter, as there is evidence to suggest that the government as a controlling shareholder can alter the firm's objectives and management profile, and may be more tempted to pursue objectives that are inconsistent with profit maximisation.[2]

Figure 5.2. Partial privatisation: Enhancing the government's credibility in the market

As part of a staged privatisation process, and to ensure success of (potential) future offerings, a few good practices should be followed by the state-owner, balancing its roles as shareholder, government owner and regulator.

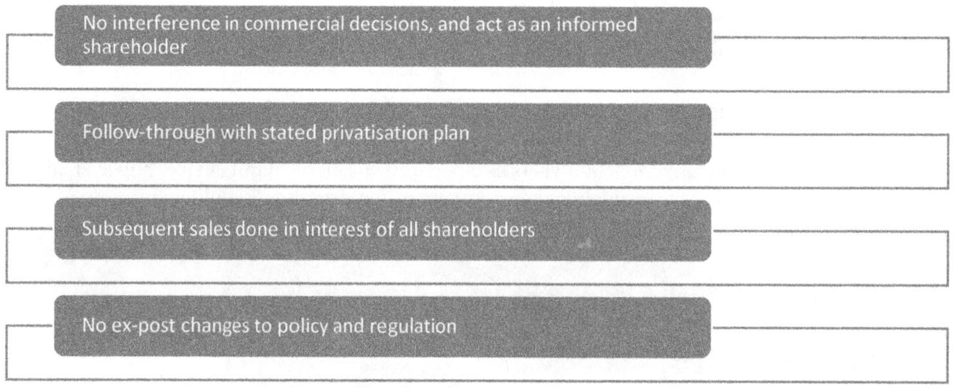

Box 5.3. OECD SOE Guidelines Chapter IV - Equitable treatment of shareholders and other investors

Where SOEs are listed or otherwise include non-state investors among their owners, the state and the enterprises should recognise the rights of all shareholders and ensure shareholders' equitable treatment and equal access to corporate information.

A. The state should strive toward full implementation of the OECD Principles of Corporate Governance when it is not the sole owner of SOEs and of all relevant sections when it is the sole owner of SOEs. Concerning shareholder protection this includes:

1. The state and SOEs should ensure that all shareholders are treated equitably.
2. SOEs should observe a high degree of transparency, including as a general rule equal and simultaneous disclosure of information, towards all shareholders.
3. SOEs should develop an active policy of communication and consultation with all shareholders.
4. The participation of minority shareholders in shareholder meetings should be facilitated so they can take part in fundamental corporate decisions such as board election.
5. Transactions between the state and SOEs, and between SOEs, should take place on market consistent terms.

B. National corporate governance codes should be adhered to by all listed and, where practical, unlisted SOEs.

C. Where SOEs are required to pursue public policy objectives, adequate information about these should be available to non-state shareholders at all times.

D. When SOEs engage in co-operative projects such as joint ventures and public-private partnerships, the contracting party should ensure that contractual rights are upheld and that disputes are addressed in a timely and objective manner.

Source: OECD (2015).

Notes

[1] Should evaluation be conducted by Parliament this could be subject to changing political environment, and thus changed perceptions as to the rationales that underpinned the decision to privatise. Appropriate risk mitigation strategies should be adopted at the outset of the process, to ensure the guiding principles, goals and rationales of the privatisation are transparent.

[2] Interestingly, Boubakri, et al. (2011) find that in developing countries, where there is a lack of an established institutional framework for efficient corporate governance, concentrated ownership is more likely to ensure the success of privatisation than in countries with low investor protection.

References

Eerste Kamer der Staten-Generaal (the Senate) (2012), "Summary of main findings of the parliamentary enquiry by the Dutch Senate into privatization and agencification of central government services", https://www.eerstekamer.nl/behandeling/20121030/lost_connections_summary_of_main.

National Audit Office (2014), "The Privatisation of Royal Mail", Report by the Comptroller and Auditor General, https://www.nao.org.uk/wp-content/uploads/2014/04/The-privatisation-of-royal-mail.pdf.

National Audit Office (2018), "The return of Lloyd's Banking Group to private ownership", Report by the Comptroller and Auditor General, https://www.nao.org.uk/wp-content/uploads/2018/06/The-return-of-Lloyds-Banking-Group-to-private-ownership.pdf

OECD (2015), *OECD Guidelines on Corporate Governance of State-Owned Enterprises*, 2015 Edition, OECD Publishing, Paris. http://dx.doi.org/10.1787/9789264244160-en

OECD (2003), *Privatising State-Owned Enterprises: An Overview of Policies and Practices in OECD Countries*, OECD Publishing, Paris, https://doi.org/10.1787/9789264104099-en.

Seven, B. (2001), "Legal Aspects of Privatisation: A Comparative Study of European Implementations", Universal Publishers.com.

Annex A. Ensuring anti-corruption and integrity in the privatisation process: A step-by-step guide

Step: Establishment of guiding principles

Main corruption risk: Undue influence or bribery leading to the wrong decision to privatise or the wrong asset identified for privatisation

Stage	Select red flags	Select questions to be asked
Identifying and articulating policy objectives (good practices in Chapter 2)	Opacity in the rationale for privatisation / Unclear, inaccessible or irrational objectives for divestment Absence or manipulation of assessments used to inform the decision-making process (e.g. competition, value for money, allocation of funding).	Are objectives well justified and clear? What tools were used to inform the decision-making process? Did they include a sound assessment of risks prone to the sector, including corruption risks? Are there mechanisms to assess the accuracy and reliability of the decision-making process?
Establishing a transparent and credible institutional framework (good practices in Chapter 2)	No centralised ownership agency or function to steer the process No safeguards to ensure integrity in the process	Are decisions made amongst a few or in an opaque way? Are there adequate mechanisms and safeguards in place, including claims channels for complaints? How soon were external auditors involved in the process?

Step: Measures before divesting

Main corruption risk: Manipulation or abuse of the methods undertaken prior to divestment that grant immediate benefit or facilitate the future diversion of rents by corrupt actors.

Stage	Select red flags	Select questions to be asked
Appropriately staging the privatisation process (good practices in Chapter 3)	Unclear or irrational decisions about how much of the enterprise is to be sold and in which stages (taking note of cases where partial privatisation leaves company vulnerable to government interference and where risk and benefits are not fully transferred to private sector) Unclear or irrational decisions about the timing of sales	Were decisions about staging privatisation well informed? Does the process seem rushed?
Pre-privatisation industry restructuring (Chapter 3)	Sped-up timeframe combined with lacking structural separation (e.g. selloff of monopoly without a sound regulatory framework) Restructuring of the company and market may have benefitted a particular actor or group Low regulatory capacity and weak enforcement	Will bidders be offered a monopolistic position in the post-privatisation market? Were adequate competition, or anti-trust regulations and effective enforcement mechanisms in place? Or, if not, was there sufficient time for them to be developed?
Pre-privatisation company restructuring (Chapter 3)	No or little due diligence on the asset selected for privatisation (e.g. ignorance to sanctions or previous infractions); or failed due diligence test Signs of basic governance weaknesses within the SOE (e.g. issues at board level, non-transparent appointment processes of board members or executive management) Questions about the accuracy and validity of company documents and accounts (e.g. unreliable internal audit or audits that point to irregularities) Previous company history with sanctions or irregularities or history of business with sanctioned entities Evidence that company managers or employees take advantage of the restructuring process to strip assets	Is there full disclosure of the potential risks (including corruption risks) posed for the buyer? Are practices of financial and non-financial disclosure, and accounting up to international standards? Is there an integrated system of internal control and risk management? Autonomous and capacitated internal audit? Did employees and management of the company act in a way that supports the integrity of the process? Were any privileged allocations given to employees or managers announced publicly in advance?
Deciding on appropriate method of sale (good practices in Chapter 3)	Selected transaction mode is more inherently opaque than others (e.g. management buyouts versus IPOs, respectively) Process timelines are sped up (e.g. to avoid checks and balances; no time for development of specialised regulation for monopolies)	Were other methods of sale evaluated? What criteria did the seller use to decide on the appropriate method of sale? Is there sufficient time afforded for the capacity-building needed?

Step: Organising the process of privatisation

Main corruption risk: Collusion, bid-rigging and/or bribery affecting the pricing and criteria of sale, and/or the awarding of the sale to an inappropriate buyer

Stage	Select red flags	Select questions to be asked
Best practices for drawing upon external advice (good practices in Chapter 4)	No conflict of interest management in utilising external advisors Apparent or real conflicts of interest of external advisors	Were the good practices outlined in 4.2 used in the selection and work of external advisors? Was there a thorough assessment of the need for contractors and was the process competitive?
Determining company valuation and establishing sound pricing methods (good practices in Chapter 4)	Falsified/doctored sale criteria (e.g. cost, or requirements for quality and deliverables) Contractual terms misaligned with previous objectives (e.g. possible tailoring of criteria for specific bidders)	Have risks and liabilities been calculated in the sale price? Was the sale price based on sound assumptions, arrived at independently of the buyer and company? Was it a used as a guide for the vendor in appraising bids? Were there price hikes or reductions following the initial pricing?
Determining potential buyers and handing bids (good practices in Chapter 4)	Lack of justification if/where non-competitive procedures are used in bidding Selection criteria is not objectively defined and not established in advance (e.g. seemingly tailored to a specific bidder) Signs of bid-rigging or collusion in the bidding process Lack of due diligence regarding the buyer (e.g. undeclared conflicts of interest or infractions, unreasonable business plan)	To what extent did the state draw attention to promote the opportunity for purchase? Was there more than one bid? Are the evaluators of bids familiar with the bidders? Is there any evidence that would-be bidders were bribed or blackmailed to avoid participating? Has proper due diligence been carried out on the buyer? If another company or group, is the ultimate beneficial owner known? Were there specific criteria to select a preferred bidder, and were they used in the selection of the winning bidder? Did the winning bidder meet specification requirements and have a reasonable business plan (especially in the case of assets that are in the process of liquidation or are distressed)?

Step: Steps to be taken post-privatisation

Main corruption risk: Evading accountability of the privatisation process and stifling oversight in the subsequent allocation of proceeds and delivery of contractual terms

Stage	Select red flags	Select questions to be asked
Accountability and transparency in handling privatisation proceeds (good practices in Chapter 5)	No rules in privatisation legislation on method of payment expected from the investor (e.g. leaving room for ambiguity or confusion in payment scheme) Use of proceeds not determined in the legal decision triggering the selloff. Absence of accounting records that can be verified by external assessment	Do public accounts adequately reflect the sale proceeds, residual assets or remaining liabilities? Are processes in place to assess the immediate and/or eventual spending of the proceeds received by the state (particularly if diverted to public policy goals)?
Systematically conducting post-privatisation evaluation (good practices in Chapter 5)	Inexistent or inadequate evaluation on the compliance with contractual terms or performance (e.g. potential that evaluators are not independent and ignore non-compliance or underperformance)	Is post-privatisation evaluation conducted? Are there any potential conflicts of interests on the part of the evaluators? Have any irregularities been detected and, if so, addressed by the appropriate authorities?
Subjecting the transaction to an ex-post audit process (good practices in Chapter 5)	Inexistent or inadequate internal audit (e.g. potential that auditors are forced or paid to ignore signs of influence)	Were there any allegations of improper practices during the process? Were they investigated? Was the transaction subject to independent, external audit? If so, were external auditors selected in a transparent and credible way? Was the audit comprehensive, including audit of the transaction itself and disbursement of funds?

Annex B. Key questions for policy makers

The OECD has developed this guide as a tool support the implementation of the *Guidelines on Corporate Governance of State-Owned Enterprises* ("OECD SOE Guidelines"). The Guide is organised in the form of a manual on the step-by-step process of conducting a privatisation from start to finish. It is primarily addressed to the entities responsible for the state-ownership function or entities or which are responsible for orchestrating the privatisation process. These key questions should be answered by policy makers for each stage of the privatisation process before embarking on an individual transaction or full-scale privatisation programme.[1]

Stage 1: Guiding principles that should inform policy makers considering undertaking a privatisation process

Step 1.1 Identify and articulate policy objectives

- Is there a clear rationale for embarking on the privatisation process? Have the concerned policy makers weighed the various trade-offs, considered value-for-money, conducted a cost-benefit analysis, and evaluated potential Impact on public service delivery (if applicable)?
- Is there adequate competition and market regulation in place prior to the privatisation? If not, has the government devised a plan to undertake market restructuring before the privatisation?
- Is the rationale for privatisation consistent with the state ownership policy?
- Has the government clearly identified how privatisation proceeds will be used?

Step 1.2: Establish a transparent and credible institutional framework with high-level political support

- Does the privatisation programme/transaction benefit from high-level political support?
- Is there a clear institutional framework in place that ensures a whole-of-government dialogue?
- Has the ownership entity (or other competent authority) been assigned as "project manager" and to steer the process?
- Is the ownership entity independent, competent, well resourced, and subject to high standards of accountability and transparency?
- For individual transactions, has a steering group or equivalent coordination group been set up involving the owner, key members of the SOE management team and ideally a couple members of the board of the company?
- Has the ownership entity identified key stakeholders to the process?

Step 1.3: Sequencing the process to build credibility and support

- Does the ownership entity have a clear idea as to the sequencing for the transaction? For example, is the concerned enterprise merely a candidate for privatisation? Will the state retain shares in the company? If so, does it plan to remain a long-term investor or does it plan to exit the company? Is this consistent with the stated rationales and sale objectives?
- Are there specific policy objectives that must be taken into consideration? For example, does the SOE operate in a strategic industry, or in an area relevant to national security that should be taken into account when sequencing the process?

Stage 2: Measures to be undertaking prior to divestment by both the company and public authorities to ensure success of the transaction

Step 2.1: Going from privatisation candidate to triggering the sell-off

- Is a specific legal act required to trigger the sell-off? If so, does this require going to parliament?
- If a larger privatisation programme is envisaged, is there a broader framework legislation that needs to be enacted?
- Have the appropriate stakeholders been adequately consulted and communicated with prior to enacting any legal acts?
- Is there a framework in place to simplify the decision-making, which might help to speed-up transactions when there is sufficient rationale, transparency and consensus around the government's privatisation priorities?

Step 2.2: Appropriately staging the privatisation process

- At the request of the ownership entity, has the management conducted a "readiness" test to ensure that the company has its "house in order"? This will include: ensuring that it has the appropriate corporate governance structures, strategy, reporting framework, transparency, capital structure and non-commercial objectives.
- Have transaction-related factors such as the size of the asset, the absorptive capacity of the market, market structure and the existence of an adequate regulatory capacity been adequately assessed?

Step 2.3: Pre-privatisation industry restructuring

- Is there anti-trust regulation to ensure competition where feasible, and specialised regulation to oversee activities where an element of monopoly is likely to persist?
- If monopoly activities necessarily remain has the government decided whether to structurally separate the monopoly into various commercial and non-commercial components?
- If the company is to remain vertically integrated during and after privatisation, is there independent and well-resourced regulation in place?
- Has a means of assuring universal policy obligations post privatisation been established?
- Has pre-privatisation restructuring been done in line with relevant rules or regulations concerning state aid (where applicable)?

Step 2.4. Pre-privatisation company restructuring, legal changes and other factors

- Has a "readiness" review been conducted to ensure that the company is fit for privatisation? Has it taken into consideration the key areas including is corporate performance, strategy, operations; management and employee questions; financial, legal and regulatory issues?
- Has the ownership entity consulted with the company board and management on its readiness for privatisation?
- Has an external advisor been appointed to work with the company should any restructuring be required?
- Have key issues relating to the scope and role of the state-owner been considered? For example regarding the rate-of-return requirements; dividend policy; and future liabilities, which might affect decisions taken by the board and management with, regard to the company's capital structure.

Step 2.5. Addressing employee and stakeholder relationships and concerns

- Have the situation of SOEs employees post-privatisation been considered? Are these in line with national labour laws and civil service codes (where applicable)?
- Have the appropriate steps been taken to dialogue with labour representation? This includes information at an early stage; consultation with through existing institutional arrangements; and if necessitated, negotiation on potential measures to be taken.
- Has the board and management developed a consultation and communication plan in consultation with a communications advisor to ensure that stakeholders are adequately informed of the process, at the right stages?
- Should specific measures be warranted have they been analysed and any financial liabilities or other residual liabilities been accounted for in advance?

Step 2.6: Deciding on the appropriate method of sale

- Has the privatisation method taken into account the size of the enterprise to be sold, market conditions and the objectives of the process?
- Have the merits and demerits of various privatisation methods been considered, including the relative costs and benefits?
- Has the government revisited its sequencing and staging decisions to ensure that it is coherent with the chosen privatisation method?

Stage 3: Organisation of the privatisation process

Step 3.1 Effectively steering the process to see through the transaction

- Has the state-ownership entity or other assigned entity to oversee the transaction established an organ (typically a steering group and a project group) to oversee the privatisation transaction? Does this involve the appropriate set of stakeholders?
- Has the relative roles and responsibilities of various stakeholders involved been clearly defined for each stage of the process?

Step 3.2 Best practices for drawing up on external advice

- Have external advisors been hired at a very early stage in the process? Has special care been taken to ensure that the firms were selected based on a competitive process and evaluated for potential conflicts of interest and selected according to their quality, competence, and experience?
- Has the separation of advisory and sale mandates been ensured to reduce the likelihood of conflicts of interest?
- Has special care been taken to ensure that the advisors and the SOE have not hired the same firm? Has the ownership entity received assurances that the advisor is only representing the government or its selling agent's interests?
- Has the in-house expertise in the ownership/privatisation unit/agency been cultivated to be able to have an informed dialogue with external advisors on key questions related to the transaction (e.g. valuation or staging, etc.)?
- Has the fee and incentives structures of advisors been carefully considered?

Step 3.3 Determining company valuation

- Has the ownership entity established a valuation based on the principle of "fair market value"?
- Has the valuation fed into the decision-making on the sales method, or sequencing of the sale?
- Who is responsible for establishing the valuation? If an external advisor is involved has the role of valuation been separated from the sales mandate to ensure there is no conflict of interest? If a special commission has been established in the government has care been taken to ensure that members are sufficiently independent and qualified to make an informed opinion?
- Has the government set a "reservation price" for the sale?
- Has the selected valuation methodology reflect the qualities and characteristics of the asset?
- Has the company provided enough information to make an informed decision on its valuation?

Step 3.4 Determining potential buyers and handling bids

- Has a set of pre-qualification criteria been established to select a future buyer should multiple bidders be considered for the sale?
- Have appropriate safeguards been established to ensure that bids are handled transparently, while respecting confidentiality, and selected according to the sales objectives set at the start of the process?
- If specific national security or public interest considerations are at hand, has the government thought through the means through which it wishes to protect those interests? Has its strategic interests been made transparent and

disclosed, and the means through which it protects them proportionate?

- Has the government carried out due diligence of the potential buyer's track record in ethics, tax, human rights, labour practices and other areas of concern?
- Have bids been handled transparently, while respecting confidentiality, to avoid irregular practices? Do potential bidders have right to recourse in case their rights have been violated?
- Has information exchange with potential bidders been subject to confidentiality agreements?

Step 3.5 Active and on-going communication

- Has the ownership entity devised a pro-active communication plan for all stages of the privatisation process? This includes communication with various stakeholders both internal to the government, with parliament; with the company and its management and employees and with stakeholders and the general public.
- Has a risk mitigation strategy been put in place should the transaction lack some public support?

Stage 4: Issues to consider post-privatisation

Step 4.1 Handling residual guarantees or liabilities

- Has the framework or privatisation legislation specified how the public authority involved in executing the transaction should defray costs, including debt write-offs resulting from balance sheet adjustments?
- Have these been handled appropriately and according to the stated process following the sale?

Step 4.2 Accountability and transparency in handling privatisation proceeds

- Has the legal decision triggering the sell off identified the use for privatisation proceeds?
- Have the proceeds been handled to ensure a high level of accountability and transparency?

Step 4.3 Systematically conducting post-privatisation evaluation

- Has a competent body been assigned with evaluating the transaction ex-post? This should evaluate assessment of corporate efficiency, effects on markets and stakeholders, as well as the impact on consumers, especially where public service delivery is concerned.

Step 4.4 Subjecting the transaction to an ex-post audit process

- Is there an entity responsible for carrying out an ex-post audit of the transaction? The audit should take into account propriety and value for money, and the achievement of other goals and objectives set out as part of the sales objectives.
- Have results of the audit been communicated to the public?

Step 4.5 Good governance practices in the case of partial privatisation

- If golden share are retained, are they limited to cases where they are strictly necessary (and in line with applicable legislation) to protect certain essential public interests such as those relating to the protection of public security and proportionate to the pursuit of these objectives?
- Are protections for minority shareholders laid down in the relevant legislation and/or listing requirements?

Notes

[1] The focus is on transactions that result in the full or partial privatisation of enterprises involved in economic activities, and where the privatisation results in a significant change in the degree of control exercised by the state if it remains shareholder.

ORGANISATION FOR ECONOMIC CO-OPERATION AND DEVELOPMENT

The OECD is a unique forum where governments work together to address the economic, social and environmental challenges of globalisation. The OECD is also at the forefront of efforts to understand and to help governments respond to new developments and concerns, such as corporate governance, the information economy and the challenges of an ageing population. The Organisation provides a setting where governments can compare policy experiences, seek answers to common problems, identify good practice and work to co-ordinate domestic and international policies.

The OECD member countries are: Australia, Austria, Belgium, Canada, Chile, the Czech Republic, Denmark, Estonia, Finland, France, Germany, Greece, Hungary, Iceland, Ireland, Israel, Italy, Japan, Korea, Latvia, Lithuania, Luxembourg, Mexico, the Netherlands, New Zealand, Norway, Poland, Portugal, the Slovak Republic, Slovenia, Spain, Sweden, Switzerland, Turkey, the United Kingdom and the United States. The European Union takes part in the work of the OECD.

OECD Publishing disseminates widely the results of the Organisation's statistics gathering and research on economic, social and environmental issues, as well as the conventions, guidelines and standards agreed by its members.

OECD PUBLISHING, 2, rue André-Pascal, 75775 PARIS CEDEX 16
ISBN 978-92-64-60580-0 – 2019

www.ingramcontent.com/pod-product-compliance
Lightning Source LLC
Chambersburg PA
CBHW061222240926
51846CB00006B/1321